Kathryn courageously and candidly shares ╵ breakdown to breakthrough. She supplem others become their own best friend. If yc self-esteem or confidence, this book is for y ‿‿ ʋıg as the Australian Outback…Kathryn helps yoᵤ ‿‿ᵗ on track towards reaching your full potential.

An essential text for anyone, whether you struggle with confidence and self esteem or already firmly believe in yourself. Kathryn gives refreshingly honest, caring yet direct advice on self talk, the friends we choose, and transformational language. This practical guide offers clear steps for behavioral and attitudinal change so you see immediate results. Highly recommended.

Are you sometimes your own worst enemy? Do you have that critical voice inside your head that puts you down and holds you back from achieving your goals? Then this is the book for you. Step by step you will learn where that voice came from and more importantly how to re-program it and turn it into your own personal cheer squad.

"Kathryn Orford's Become Your #1 Fan is powerful and inspiring. As a Confidence Coach, she has encouraged people for decades to become more confident, self-aware and compassionate. This new book furthers her transformative and loving work. I am thrilled to endorse Kathryn and her book, and I know it will serve many in their growth, empowerment and interconnectedness."

Lani Kwon, MA
Founder of The Creating CoPOWERment® Center LLC
Author of The Creating CoPOWERment® Workbook:
Embracing the Power of Positive Psychology, Healing
Stories and Explorations to Create the Life You Want ©2013
published by Balboa Press, a Division of Hay House, Inc.
www.coPOWERment.com

"As a fitness professional and entrepreneur I am delighted to recommend and endorse this book for anyone, of any age, in every stage of their life. This book is equipped with amazing tools that help enrich and develop lives.

I first had the pleasure of meeting Kathryn in December of 2011, as she had sought out my expertise in health and fitness. Little did I know that I would be the one benefiting from our sessions. Kathryn's diverse range of knowledge and skill set for getting positive results through a positive balanced mindset helped me develop my own coaching style and better elicit results with my clients.

This book is filled with powerful personal challenges setting the path to personal development and inner enrichment!

Great job Kathryn I am proud to have you as a client and friend!"

Bryan Watkins
Fitness Professional and Owner of Watkins Fitness LLC

ENDORSEMENTS

Finally after all the buzz on "The Law of Attraction", Kathryn Orford gives us the missing link. The key to becoming your #1 Fan, developing your self-worth & really believing in your dreams. In this life-changing book Kathryn provides the tools to produce results by developing your worthiness and learning to truly love yourself. And there in lies the real "secret" to manifesting all of your dreams. This book is a game changer.

Cellular Memory Expert, Best-Selling Author and International Speaker Dr. Sugar Singleton Marcy, is a practicing medical doctor, a loving wife and mother, and a powerful resource for women and their well being.

Kathryn walks her talk and is such an inspiration to everyone she meets. She makes her dreams a reality and is brilliant at teaching her clients to do likewise. In this inspirational story Kathryn shares how she rebuilt her life after suffering from a Nervous Breakdown that left her feeling suicidal.

Each chapter is jam packed with exercises, tools and techniques to forever change how you feel about yourself and your ability to create the life you've always dreamt of.

Sam Cawthorn
International Speaker and Best Selling Author of Boun
Forward ~ How to Transform Crisis into S
www.samcaw+

"Kathryn's deeply personal confession dissolves the stigma of self-judgment and low self-worth. Her intuitive wisdom, combined with her mentoring tools, make this book a portable coach to take with you wherever you go, most especially when you are needing inspiration or simply a reminder of who you are and why you are valuable. The pain of low self-worth can be healed and transformed. Thank you, Kathryn, for sharing your healing journey in this profound and practical book!"

Baeth Davis
International Speaker, Mentor CEO of YourPurpose.com

Become Your #1 Fan ~ How to Silence your Inner Critic and Live the Life of your Dreams is a wonderful book for anyone who wants to grow in self-confidence, overcome negative early programming, and create a life of abundance, accomplishment and joy. Author Kathryn Orford comes from a dual background, in the arts and in personal development. In her thirties, after a painful breakup, she fell into a deep depression. As she healed, she began to share her hard won understanding and growth with clients.

I found the section on understanding and overcoming fear to be particularly powerful. The book is full of exercises that are fun and enlightening, as well as profoundly transformative. Kathryn has also created rituals that touch the soul of the reader. If you are ready to move ahead to the next level in your life, I highly recommend Become Your #1 Fan.

Jillian Coleman Wheeler is an author, counselor and mentor for clients who want to change their lives. Her website is: JillianColemanWheeler.com.

I am truly blessed to have worked with Kathryn. She saved my life when I needed it the most. I was able to relate to Kathryn and her story. She was so intuitive about my needs and how to access my inner strength. The tools that she has shared and taught me are valuable life long lessons that can be carried over in all aspects of my life. I am so overjoyed that these tools are now available for any and all that choose to enhance their lives. After reading this book your life will never be the same. I really have become my own #1 Fan and I couldn't have done it without Kathryn. Thank-you.

Kim Watkins

I have had the pleasure of knowing Kathryn Orford both personally and professionally for over 5 years. She is amazingly intuitive and has been a wonderful support to me. Her presentations are sensational, interactive and fun. She connects with her audience, relates to all ages and really walks her talk. Funny, sensitive and compassionate, Kathryn is the whole package. I love her energy and spirit and consider her to be one of the wisest women I know. So I'm sure you'll benefit greatly from reading this book.

Maria Cucinotta, International Speaker. Femme
International, Sydney Australia

About the Author

Even as a small child Kathryn had the ability to chunk down the skills she'd learnt and pass them on to her friends. For example once she'd learnt how to ice skate, she was able to teach her friends to do likewise 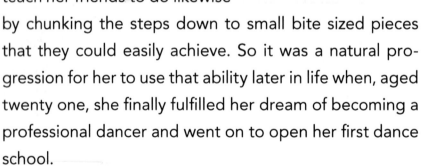 by chunking the steps down to small bite sized pieces that they could easily achieve. So it was a natural progression for her to use that ability later in life when, aged twenty one, she finally fulfilled her dream of becoming a professional dancer and went on to open her first dance school.

Her life has taken many twists and turns since then. One pivotal moment was when she was thirty-three years old and suffered a nervous breakdown. She now views her breakdown as a breakthrough to who she really was.

Her journey since then has been all about learning to love herself (warts and all) and creating the life of her dreams.

Kathryn is now known as The Confidence Coach, and has dedicated the last twenty five years to empowering people to believe in themselves and their abilities. She has trained with the world's leading authorities in human behaviour and potential. And nothing lights her up more than witnessing her clients produce results they had only previously dreamt of.

She is in demand as a Speaker, Coach, Trainer and Personal Development Facilitator.

Born and raised in Sydney Australia, Kathryn now resides in Honolulu with her teenage daughter. She's speaks and runs Become your #1 Fan Workshops for adults, children and teenagers, as well as Re-Ignite your Goddess Within Retreats for women. In any one year Kathryn takes on a handful of coaching clients and runs a VIP 6 Month Immersion Program for successful women/ goddesses ready to take their lives to the next level.

Connect with Kathryn:

Websites: www.becomeyournumberonefan.com
www.theconfidencecoach.net

Become Your #1 Fan

How to Silence Your Inner Critic and Live the Life of Your Dreams

KATHRYN ORFORD

BALBOA.
PRESS

A DIVISION OF HAY HOUSE

Balboa Press books may be ordered through booksellers or by contacting:

Balboa Press
A Division of Hay House
1663 Liberty Drive
Bloomington, IN 47403
www.balboapress.com
1 (877) 407-4847

Because of the dynamic nature of the Internet, any web addresses or links contained in this book may have changed since publication and may no longer be valid. The views expressed in this work are solely those of the author and do not necessarily reflect the views of the publisher, and the publisher hereby disclaims any responsibility for them.

The author of this book does not dispense medical advice or prescribe the use of any technique as a form of treatment for physical, emotional, or medical problems without the advice of a physician, either directly or indirectly. The intent of the author is only to offer information of a general nature to help you in your quest for emotional and spiritual well-being. In the event you use any of the information in this book for yourself, which is your constitutional right, the author and the publisher assume no responsibility for your actions.

Any people depicted in stock imagery provided by Thinkstock are models, and such images are being used for illustrative purposes only. Certain stock imagery © Thinkstock.

Printed in the United States of America.

ISBN: 978-1-4525-8474-4 (sc)
ISBN: 978-1-4525-8476-8 (hc)
ISBN: 978-1-4525-8475-1 (e)

Library of Congress Control Number: 2013918497

Balboa Press rev. date: 12/10/2013

Table of Contents

Preface

At some stage in our lives we're bound to experience a defining moment. That moment when a person, a place or an experience changes the course of our lives forever. For me that moment came in my early thirties.

It took being dumped by "the man of my dreams" to escalate my journey of self discovery. At the time, I couldn't understand how being dumped had catapulted me into the biggest blackest hole of depression. Where had the confident, successful, happy young woman gone? And who was this strange negative person who had taken over my body and mind?

You see I had been running an extremely successful school of performing arts, had a great group of friends and was happy and content with where my life was headed.

Unfortunately, not only did he cheat on me and blatantly lie to my face when I confronted him about it, he also married the "other women" within about three months of dumping me.

To say I was heart-broken was a gross understatement.

It felt as though he had ripped my heart out of my chest, thrown it onto the ground and stomped all over it. With every breath I took I could feel my life force draining from my body. My adrenal glands were all that was keeping me going.

At the time, I didn't know that I was adopted, so I had no idea his actions had triggered my "abandonment issues" big time! All I knew was that I felt completely unlovable and worthless.

To make matters worse, he and his new wife and I were all enrolled in a six-month training course. And guess who's Study Group I was in? You guessed it..... theirs! Talk about masochistic!

Looking back, I don't know why I didn't ask to be switched to another group; perhaps a sick part of me still wanted to be part of his inner circle.

Not surprisingly, every time I saw them together it felt as if my heart was being battered and bruised all over again. Somehow I managed to limp through that six months and complete the course. But it wasn't long after that, that I spiralled down into the deepest, darkest, depression.

Every ounce of my "I'm not good enough demons" reared their ugly heads and it felt as though they were literally strangling me! Day by day, I'd gear up with my suit of armour pretending everything was fine but deep down inside, I was hurting like crazy and far from fine!

One moment I was a confident, vivacious, young woman in her early thirties, full of life and positive anticipation, running an incredibly successful school of performing arts. Then suddenly I felt totally worthless. My self-esteem plummeted. I began to doubt my ability to do anything well. I couldn't choreograph anything that was remotely okay, or even think coherently for too long. I felt like a complete failure!

I remember one day while walking out into my back garden, all I could see were caterpillars and snails eating the flowers and leaves. My previous "rose coloured glasses" approach to life had disappeared, only to be replaced by a "murky pair of black lenses." It was as if the firm ground that I'd previously stood on had turned into quicksand. Every day I slipped deeper and deeper below the surface until I could barely breathe. My world became incredibly dark and lonely.

The scariest thing by far was when I turned on music and felt nothing. Music had given me such joy in the past, and developing choreography was how I connected with my essence and expressed my true spirit, but those exquisite feelings had totally disappeared, only to be replaced by feelings of complete apathy and NUMBNESS!

At one point, I got to the stage where I didn't want to get out of bed. When I did get out of bed, I would be overwhelmed by anxiety attacks at the thought of having to teach my dance classes.

Although close friends and family kept telling me to look for the light at the end of the tunnel, I assure you, there was no light in my tunnel; it was pitch black! And unfortunately, their well-meaning comments just made me feel even more isolated.

After soldiering on for a few more months, the pain became altogether unbearable. I woke up one morning and decided I couldn't stand it anymore. It was time for me to "check out" and commit suicide.

That afternoon, I went to visit my parents for what I thought was the final time. When I left, I remember looking back at their front door and telepathically sending them a message saying "thank you and please forgive me."

Somehow, I mustered up enough energy to teach my dance classes for the day. My last class was one of my favourites—my beautiful 10 year olds' Competition Team. Somehow I got through their class, and as they started leaving the studio I also telepathically sent them a message saying, "thank you for all the joy you've brought me, please forgive me and please keep dancing."

As the remaining students were disappearing out the door, I fell heavily on the polished wooden floor and sobbed deeply. A few students heard my cries and rushed back to see what was wrong. I reassured them by saying something like, "oh I'll be okay; I'm just having a tough time in my private life," before ushering them quickly back out the door.

Somehow despite my agony, I managed to drive home. On arrival I went straight to my bathroom to find the anti-depressants I planned to pour down my throat but thankfully, I couldn't find the bottle. In fact I couldn't even find the prescription. You see I'd never planned on taking them. I'd only really gone to the doctors to appease my mother, who was worried sick about me.

I continued rifling through the bathroom cupboards and drawers trying to find something that would do the trick, but since I'd always preferred homeopathic to traditional medicine, I couldn't find anything remotely capable of killing me. The entire situation would have been comical had I not been on the verge of suicide.

So once again I fell in a heap on the cold bathroom tiles sobbing hysterically. The critical voice in my head reared its ugly self, berating me mercilessly: "you're so pathetic!" "You can't even organise your own suicide properly!"

I was curled up in a foetal position, rocking myself back and forth, on those cold bathroom tiles, listening to the deep primal sounds coming from somewhere deep inside of me when the phone rang. There was no way I was about to get off the floor and answer it, so I let it ring out.

But it rang again, and again. The third time the phone rang, a gentler voice inside of me said "get up and answer it." I think I was worried that something bad might have happened to my mum or dad. So I slowly unfolded my wasted body and picked up the phone just before it rang out for the third time.

One of my beautiful students' mothers was on the line. She said uncertainly, "Are you okay?" When her daughter had come home from class, she'd told her mother how upset I was. I responded, "no, but I will be." And in that instant she read between the lines and realised what I meant. So she said "I'm in the middle of cooking dinner, but I want you to promise me you won't do anything? I'll be there in 20 mins." I knew the only way to end the call was to agree; however, I had no intention of keeping my promise. All I wanted to do was get off the phone and come up with Plan B.

I realised I'd have to move quickly and leave the house before she arrived. As I grabbed my car keys and walked towards the front door I remember saying to myself, "oh well, you'll have to drive your car off a cliff. I hope you can get that right, and not end up a paraplegic!"

Much to my surprise, just as I was about to open the front door, someone rang the doorbell. Standing there was another one of my student's parents, with a huge bouquet of beautiful flowers in her arms. She said, "We know you're going through a rough time at the moment, so we want you to know how much we love you."

At that precise moment I remembered an analogy Robert Kiyosaki had shared with us in the first personal development course I'd attended, "$ & U." He said that in life when we're off track, we'll often get a tap on the shoulder to alert us. If we ignore the first tap, the second one will be much harder. And if we don't listen to that one, next thing we know, we are flat on our backs with the smell of diesel filling our lungs and the Mack Truck tread marks across our belly, wondering what the f— hit us!

As I stood dumbfounded in my doorway with the flowers in my arms, I thought "maybe I'm not meant to go after all? I've just received two taps on the shoulder. He doesn't love you, but lots of other people do, so maybe it's time for you to learn to love yourself from the inside out instead of constantly searching for outside acknowledgement that you're okay."

In that very moment I made a pledge to myself: I promised that I would never feel that bad about myself ever again. I would never allow anyone to rob me of my self- esteem. When I made that pledge, the real work began. Was it easy? Gosh no! Was it worth it? Absolutely!

I now know that what I thought was my biggest nightmare, actually turned out to be my "biggest gift."

Some would say I suffered a nervous breakdown. But I call it my "Break Down to Breakthrough" to the real me! In that moment that I chose life, I chose to build myself up, brick by brick, day by day; to be the confident, happy woman that I am today!

Honestly, I wouldn't change a thing! It's been an amazing journey so far. Since my "Breakthrough Moment" 25 years ago, I have immersed myself in learning everything I can about how to feel great about myself. I've had the pleasure of studying with the world's leading authorities on self-esteem, self-belief and human potential. And I now consider myself to be one of them.

What I learnt as I clawed my way out of that big black hole, is that we all have our own version of "I'm not good enough." Its just that some of us are better at disguising it than others.

Acknowledgements

Twenty five years ago one book in particular provided me with the skills to start rebuilding my life and start my journey of self love and self acceptance and that was Louise Hay's Bestseller " You can Heal your Life."

I'm also incredibly grateful to all of the Personal and Professional Development Trainers, Coaches and Facilitators that have shared their wisdom, knowledge and skills with me. Robert Kiyosaki, Anthony Robbins, Robert Pante, Stephanie Burns, Marvin Oka, Michael Wall Phillipa Bond, Mahni and Geoff Dugan, Noel Posus to name a few.

I have so many people to thank. To Brooke and Lynne Hendrick and Vanessa and Kate Atwood. You were there for me in my darkest hour and without your love I may not be here today. To Ann Maree Rados and Susan Kroening for gently cradling me as I took baby steps out of my big black hole. To Ross Penman for the wonderful acupuncture sessions that resurrected my Life Force Energy. To Penny Mullen who lovingly covered my classes every time an anxiety attack left me paralysed with fear. And to all of my beautiful dance students and their families who stood by me when I was too vulnerable to teach, choreograph or be there for you.

To my late parents Rex and Muriel Orford. Your never ending love and support was the wind beneath my wings. You taught me to dream big and make my dreams a reality. And to my biological parents, thank you for giving me the the "biggest gift" of all ~ my life.

A huge thank you also to my Speaker Buddies who support me and inspire me to continue sharing my story and play a "Bigger Game." Especially Sam Cawthorn.

It takes a lot of courage to share your most vulnerable moments, so a huge thank you to Peter, Kim, Haneef and Lisa for sharing their stories of how they didn't allow their past to dictate their future.

And a huge shout out and mahalo to Dr Allison E. Paynter for your invaluable input on how best to arrange my content along with your expertise editing my suicide story. And Andrew and Kimberly Arakawa from Prune Copywriting for your expertise delivered in a true aloha spirit.

Thank you to Kerry Crow from Crow Designs for creating the images throughout the book.

Finally a big thank you to my beautiful daughter Samara for your patience as this book became a reality. You are without a doubt the biggest gift in my life. You light up my world and I am so proud to be your mum!

Introduction

This book is all **about EMPOWERING YOU to be the best version of you, that you can be and in the process 'Becoming your # 1 Fan.'**

Chances are, up until now you haven't been. In fact perhaps at times you've been your Worst Enemy versus your #1 Fan. At times I know I certainly was. I used to treat my friends better than I treated myself. How crazy is that? And I'll bet you've done the same thing. Have you ever stopped and wondered why we do that?

Well as you make your way through this book, you'll not only learn why, but more importantly how to stop treating yourself so badly. And how to become your best friend and #1 Fan.

I'm not talking about becoming narcissistic or big headed. I'm talking about feeling 100% comfortable with who you are and how you interact in the world. I'm talking about the amazing feeling that comes from knowing that you can rely on yourself to treat yourself with the love and respect that you really deserve.

Let's face it, how can anyone else really like and appreciate who you are, if you don't like yourself? And how can you have a healthy primary relationship if you're coming from a place of deficit and relying on someone else to top you up, tell you how special you are and make you feel complete?

For those of you that already feel reasonably confident about who you are, I guarantee you'll learn some fine distinctions on how to tweak those feelings, fine tune your beliefs and behaviours and create a success mindset that will catapult your confidence and self belief to a whole new stratosphere!

A lot of clients I've had the pleasure of working with were already reasonably successful and confident in themselves and their abilities, however most of them had a "sabotage pattern" when it came to really creating the life they dreamt of. The moment they got close to landing their dream job/role, achieving an important goal, or creating the loving relationship they craved they'd find a way to unconsciously sabotage their efforts. Can you relate?

What they discovered in working with me was that deep down inside, underneath their confident persona were some unconscious limiting beliefs and/or a lack of self esteem and self worth that was stopping them from achieving their goals/outcomes.

Words fall short in describing the buzz I get out of providing my clients with the tools to identify and then free themselves of those old limiting beliefs and sabotage patterns. I get to witness them soaring like eagles and achieving goals beyond their wildest imagination. And I've got to tell you that feels amazing!

Hence the reason I'm writing this book. I'm committed to sharing this process with as many people on this planet as possible!

What I aim to do is walk you through the same process that I share in my coaching sessions and workshops. So that you too can soar like an eagle and live the life you dreamt of (or had perhaps given up on years ago).

After 25 years of immersion, my "tool kit" is a veritable smorgasbord of techniques, mindsets and beliefs that have certainly worked for me, and they can work for you too.

Some of the key factors I've learned are:

- The difference between Self Esteem and Self Confidence?
- What is Self Esteem and Self Worth?
- How does it gets depleted, and more importantly; how we can re-build it on a daily basis?
- How can we develop Self Esteem, Self Worth, Self Confidence and Self Belief in all aspects of our lives?
- How to re-program our negative self talk and turn it into a cheer squad.

- How to Create and Maintain a Peak Performance Mindset.
- The Key to implementing the Law of Attraction to manifest your hearts desires.

And in that process, I've really learned to Become my #1 Fan. Accepting myself warts and all and really believing in my ability to create an amazing life! I no longer need everyone else's approval because I approve of myself, and I've got to tell you that feels amazing!! And if I can do it, you can too!

Do you ever find yourself:

~ Chastising yourself?
~ Playing the compare and despair game?
~ Saying yes to people when you really want to say no?
~ Listening to that critical voice that tells you you're not "enough." For example: not good enough, clever enough, attractive enough, etc....?
~ Buying into other people's limiting beliefs about your capability of being successful, happy, achieving your goals, etc...?
~ Giving up on a goal or dream after failing to achieve it?
~ Procrastinating?

~ Believing and breathing life into your "story" of why you can't do, be, have whatever you really want?

~ Allowing your past to dictate your future?

I could go on and on but I'm hoping by now you get my drift? If you could relate to any of the points above I'm sure you're going to enjoy this book. Each chapter will give you the tools to ditch your limiting beliefs and behaviours and replace them with far more empowering ones so that you can Silence your Inner Critic, Become your #1 Fan and Live the Life of your Dreams. So let's get started!

CHAPTER ONE

Let's Start at the Very Beginning

When you were born, you had an infinite amount of Self Esteem and Self Worth. Take a moment right now, and picture yourself as a tiny baby. Babies know how special and unique they are! They also know that their needs are important.

When they're hungry they let the world know, when they're tired, they broadcast it to the nation, when they're wet and uncomfortable they also let us know loud and clear. They communicate their wants, needs and desires knowing without a shadow of a doubt that they deserve to have them met.

We've all witnessed the amazing effect that babies and young animals have on the people around them. They bring out our best qualities as human beings, and have the capacity to melt even the hardest heart!

Why is that? Well I think it's because they are so inno-cent, pure and vulnerable. Being around them, rekindles something deep inside us. We reconnect with the fact that we were once that exquisite and whole!!!

Stop and think about it, have you ever heard a family member screaming at a toddler "Stand up and do it again you silly idiot" as the toddler falls over attempting to take those first few shaky steps? Of course not; we encourage them in a soft loving voice to get up and have another go, and applaud like crazy when they do something new for the first time!!

When you were born, you had more than enough self esteem to last your lifetime! The analogy I use is that when you were born, you had an infinite amount of balloons, and those balloons represented your self esteem and self worth. Unfortunately over time balloons burst based on negative comments and feedback that we receive from the people around us, and our self esteem and self worth starts to decrease.

You might be asking yourself well that's all well and good but where did those feelings go? And that's a great question.

The answer is so simple and yet so profound that when you really "get this" you'll realise that no matter what's happened in your past, or how you feel about yourself right now, you're now in control and you can take charge of your self esteem and self worth once and for all and re-build it on a daily basis. Once we take full responsibility for our self esteem and self worth, no-one can rob us of it ever again.

BECOME YOUR #1 FAN

Take a moment right now and imagine the room you're in totally filling with balloons in your favourite colour/s. Now see the balloons multiplying and filling the building you're in. Now see them floating out of the windows and down the street.

Imagine standing on the roof of your building and seeing trillions of balloons for as far as your eyes can see, and then some! That's how much Self Esteem and Self Worth you were born with!

You see somewhere between one to two years of age, you got your first piece of negative feedback and that came as a huge shock.

It might have been your parents saying "that's naughty, don't do that" or a child flicking sand in your eyes in the sandpit, or it may have been an older jealous sibling pushing you over when your parents or caretaker left the room.

Whatever it was for you, your brain was nowhere near developed enough to understand that the negative feedback was either about a behaviour you were doing, or perhaps it had nothing to do with you and was fuelled by their feelings of inadequacy. Whatever the circumstances, chances are you personalised it, and decided that you were flawed in some way.

That in turn popped one or more of your balloons, and created the foundation for self doubt!

Are you familiar with the name Jack Canfield? He's the guy that co authored all of the Chicken Soup for the Soul Books and also featured in the movie, *The Secret*. He's also one of the top Success Coaches in the world.

In 1982 Jack researched how many negative and how many positive comments a young pre-schooler receives each day. And the results were staggering.

He found that on average, a pre-school aged child received **460 negative or critical comments** and **only 75 positive or supportive comments.** Now that's both scary and very revealing!!

So in **one week** that's **3,220 negative** comments and **525 positive ones.**

In **a month** that equates to **14,260 negative** comments and **2,325 positive ones.**

Over **a year** that adds up to **171,120 negative**

comments and only **27,900 positive** comments. And by the time we're 8 years old we'll have received an average of **102,000,6720 negative** comments and only **167,400 positive ones.** Can you hear the balloons popping?????

Is it any wonder that by the time we made it to 8 years old, we had feelings of inadequacy and self doubt? "I'm not good enough" feelings lurked deep down in our unconscious minds. But we tried not to show it to the rest of the world, and in the process created a "persona" that isn't who we really are. Its more like an invisible suit of armour or mask that we wear to protect ourselves from more negative feedback. And unfortunately until we "wake up" and take charge of our self esteem and self worth we perpetuate the pattern by criticising ourselves on a daily basis.

Based on reading those stats, you could get angry and say, "How could my parents have done this to me?" But you know what? They were just doing the best they could with the knowledge and skills they had available to them. And let's face it, they probably based their parenting style on how they were parented. And their parents probably based their parenting style on how they were parented. And so it goes!!

The **great news** is that **YOU'RE IN A POSITION TO CLAIM BACK YOUR SELF ESTEEM AND SELF WORTH** and change that pattern for good.

So it's time to put on your gloves and get to work:

You're going to need a book or journal (you can buy them at most office supply shops). I encourage you to make it uniquely yours. You might like to cover it in your favourite colours and find a picture of yourself aged 6-18 months, along with one of you now and put them both on the cover. As you read the following chapters, the reason I've suggested that will become more evident.

You'll need your journal to do the Become your #1 Fan Exercises you'll find throughout the book. And I also encourage you to use it to write down your thoughts, feelings, fears and wins either on a daily or weekly basis.

Journalling is a wonderful way to track your progress. I love looking back at my old journals as they put into perspective how far I've come and how much I've developed as a human being.

Information is useless unless we put it into action! **So I highly recommend you do the exercises as you go** because then you'll be doing something every day to reclaim your self esteem and become your #1 Fan! Similar to going to the gym to build muscle strength, except in this instance you're building emotional strength and awareness.

I've created a membership website specifically to

support you as you make your way through the exercises in this book. Information is useless unless you TAKE ACTION. So I look forward to connecting with you directly. You'll also get to interact with other readers as we all share our wins, challenges and insights. And because you've bought this book you're entitled to one months free membership.

www.becomeyournumberonefan.com

Once you go to the website above click on the Members Log In Icon to set up your 1 month's free membership. When it asked you for a discount code type in: BOOK OFFER

CHAPTER TWO

What Is Self Confidence?

Self Confidence is a feeling - an inner fire and an outer radiance, a basic satisfaction with what one is, plus a reaching out to become more. Contrary to popular belief confidence is not something a few people are born with and others are not, for it is an acquired characteristic.

Confidence is the personal possession of no one; the person who has it learns it - and goes on learning. The most gifted individual on earth has to construct confidence in his or her gifts from the basis of faith and experience, like anybody else. The tools will differ from one person to the next, but the essential task is the same.

Confidence and poise are available to us all according to our abilities and needs - not somebody else's - provided we utilise our gifts and expand them.

One of the most rewarding aspects of confidence is that it sits gracefully on every age and level of life - on children, men, women, the famous, the obscure, rich, poor, artist, executive, teenager, the very old. And you can take it with you into old age.

Most people have more to work with than they realise. We refer to them as "unused excellencies" and finding and releasing this potential in ourselves is one of the major challenges of modern life.

Having self-confidence doesn't mean that a person will be able to do everything. However the great danger is not that we shall overreach our capacities, but that we shall undervalue and under-employ them, thus never realising our truest potential.

Self-confidence isn't necessarily a general character-istic that shows up in all areas of a person's life. Typically, a person will have some areas of their lives where they feel confident, e.g. school or work environment, sporting ability, relationships etc....while at the same time they may not feel as confident in other areas e.g. finances or gardening etc... However they have the confidence and ability to ask for help in areas where they lack expertise.

HOW IS SELF CONFIDENCE INITIALLY DEVELOPED?

Lots of things affect the development of self-confidence. Parents' attitudes are crucial to children's feelings about themselves, particularly in children's early years. When parents provide acceptance, children receive a solid foundation for good feelings about themselves.

If one or both parents are excessively critical or demanding, or if they are overprotective and discourage moves toward independence, children may come to believe they are incapable, inadequate, or inferior. However, if parents encourage children's moves toward self-reliance and accept and love their children when they make mistakes, children will learn to accept themselves and will be on their way to developing self-confidence.

Surprisingly, lack of self-confidence isn't necessarily related to lack of ability. Instead it's often the result of focusing too much on the unrealistic expectations or standards of others, especially parents and society.

Friends' influences can be as powerful, or more powerful, than those of parents and society in shaping feelings about one's self, especially in our teenage years.

Students in their high school years re-examine values and develop their own identities, and through this process are particularly vulnerable to the influence of friends. So if you are at this stage in your life, please take a moment to consider whether your friends encourage you to pursue the things you love, or put pressure on you to conform to the groups ideals, and in the process lose touch with who you are and let go of your hopes and dreams?

HOW DO WE RECOGNISE SELF CONFIDENCE IN OURSELVES AND OTHERS?

Self-confident people trust their own abilities, have a general sense of control in their lives, and believe that, within reason, they will be able to do what they wish, plan, and expect.

Self-confident people have expectations that are realistic. Even when some of their expectations aren't met, they continue to be positive and to accept themselves.

People who aren't self-confident depend excessively on the approval of others in order to feel good about themselves. They tend to avoid taking risks because they fear failure. Generally they don't expect to be successful. They often put themselves down and tend to discount or ignore compliments paid to them.

By contrast, self-confident people accept compliments graciously and are willing to risk the disapproval of others because they generally trust their own abilities, qualities and judgements.

Confident people feel "comfortable in their skin." They like themselves from the inside out. They tend to accept themselves warts and all, so don't rely on acknowledgement from other people to feel good about themselves.

An important key to success is self confidence. An important key to self confidence is preparation. ~ Arthur Ashe

BECOME YOUR #1 FAN

Self confidence leaves many clues. Think about someone you feel exudes Self Confidence. What tells you they're confident? How do they hold their body? How do they move? How do they communicate with others? Do they make direct eye contact with whoever they are speaking to? **What is it that tells you that this person has Self Confidence?**

Write down what you've noticed and choose one skill each week to copy? Remember that's how we learned to walk and talk. We copied everyone around us! So it's the same when we're adding a new skill to our tool kit. Pretending we're someone else or 'faking it till we make it' can initially serve us when we're acquiring a new skill, behaviour, belief or mindset. Then over time we can take ownership of it and making it uniquely ours.

WHERE DOES SELF CONFIDENCE COME FROM?

Some people are under the misconception that you're either born with confidence or you aren't. But that is simply not true!

Self-confidence isn't something people are born with. Its a skill that's developed over time. And it results from a combination of factors:

1. **Learned skill:** Self-confidence is a combination of skills, not just a single quality. People are not born with it or without it. It can be learned.
2. **Practice:** <u>Self-confidence comes from practice.</u> It may appear to be spontaneous, but it isn't.
3. **Internal locus of control:** Self-confidence results from what psychologists call an internal locus (central point) of control. This means that people who are self-directing, who accept responsibility for their own results, have greater self-confidence.

The opposite of this are people with low self confidence who tend to sit back and watch life pass them by. These people tend to believe that life is tough and out of their control. Living into this belief causes them to create more of the same e.g. a life that isn't fulfilling, a job that they don't enjoy, a relationship that is either physically or emotionally abusive, a lack of money and resources.

Some people choose to believe that they will never get ahead because of their upbringing and circumstances, but there are plenty of happy successful people who've risen above their circumstances to prove this theory wrong.

Having a vision, the drive, the determination and the courage to step out of their comfort zones took them places they could only have previously dreamt of! Did they get it right the first time? Probably not, chances are they probably made lots of mistakes along the way, but instead of looking at the mistakes as failures, they took it as feedback, made some corrections and continued to move towards their goal.

> *Nothing builds self esteem and self confidence like accomplishment ~ Thomas Carlyle*

In 1969 Neil Armstrong and the team of Apollo 11 Astronauts set off for the moon. Do you know how much of the time they were "on course?" If you're like me, I just presumed they got in their spacecraft and navigated their way to the moon. Guess what..... they didn't. 93% of the time they were "off course", which means they were only "on course for 7%" of the time. You might be wondering "so how did they get to their destination?" Well the majority of their time was spent reviewing and correcting till eventually, on July 20th, they got to their destination.

The diagram below sums it up beautifully.

And that's what achieving goals in life is all about. Its about reviewing and correcting without any form of self judgement.

As tiny children we knew how to do this, otherwise we would never have learned to walk or talk. We didn't know the meaning of the word failure or give up! Chances are when we fell over taking our first shaky steps our family clapped and propped us back up again and lovingly encouraged us to have another go. So failing back then we received applause and it was FUN! With steel determination and a sense of joy, curiosity and positive anticipation we persisted until we learned to walk and talk.

So if you did it then, you can do it again now! All you need to do is shed some of the limiting beliefs and conditioning that you've taken on board since then. And that's what this book will show you "how" to do!

CHAPTER THREE

Where Do Our Behaviours and Beliefs Come From?

If you've read the previous chapters then you can probably fathom a guess at where our beliefs and behaviours come from. If you've skipped to this chapter, I highly recommend you go back and read Chapter One and Two first.

So where do our behaviours and beliefs come from? From everyone around us; our parents, siblings, grandparents, caregivers, friends etc.....

When we emerge from the womb as tiny babies we have a lot of adjusting and learning to do. Inside the womb all of our needs were met effortlessly and easily and we didn't really have to "do" anything. Just sleep, experiment with moving our limbs and receive nourishment from our mothers' umbilical cord.

The instant we made our entrance into the big wide world everything changed. We were showered with love and more than likely, everything we did was applauded. But then we discovered that we couldn't move around like everyone else, and to top it off, we couldn't communicate like everyone else. So we soon realised we had better immerse ourselves in learning how to "be" in this brand new world. So over those first couple of years we were on a huge learning curve; learning to crawl, walk, run and talk.

Most two-year-olds understand at least 150 words and add ten new ones to their vocabulary nearly every day. By the age of six, most children have a vocabulary of nearly 13,000 words.

So much of who we are is set up in those first 5-6years. The level to which we felt loved and wanted in those early years, forms the foundation for how we feel about ourselves today.

Even if you didn't have the best of starts in life it is possible to start building your self esteem and self worth right now!

Just like when we learned to walk and talk by copying everyone around us, we also learned how to "be" in order to "fit in".

If you were the firstborn, chances are you felt extremely special and allowed a fair bit of your natural personality to emerge. If however you were the 2nd or 3rd child, you probably looked to your older sibling/s for clues on how to be and act. You may even have decided unconsciously that you would never be as clever, attractive, sporty etc. as your older sibling, so you got busy creating your own Persona to fit in.

OUR PERSONA

Our Persona is not who we really are, it's more like a mask.

What do you think yours might be? Are you the Family Clown? Or the Baby? Or perhaps the Quiet Achiever or at the opposite end of the spectrum the Mischievous One? If you were the first child you may have taken on board to be the Over Achiever or Mummy or Daddy's little Prince or Princess?

Whatever it was for you, chances are you spent a lot of time perfecting your newfound persona/role until it became who you were.

Ultimately we learn how to behave from:

- Our parents or caregivers
- Our siblings
- Other children
- Extended family and friends

We started to form beliefs about ourselves based on the feedback we received from everyone around us. If we received positive feedback it fertilised the soil for more positive beliefs to grow.

Ultimately we all received negative feedback too. And sadly our infant brains hadn't formed enough for us to realise that the feedback was just that. Feedback about a behaviour that we were doing (or not doing.) And so we personalised the feedback and started to believe we were flawed. Neurologically we're wired to look for evidence and unfortunately between two years of age and six years of age we received plenty of negative feedback.

The other thing that impacted us is how our parents/caregivers felt about themselves. If they lacked confidence or self esteem, unconsciously we mimicked them and took on board their beliefs.

Here's a wonderful poem that describes how, as children, we learn how to be based on our environment.

Children learn what they live by Dorothy Law Nolte

If a child lives with criticism, they learn to condemn.
If a child lives with hostility, they learn to fight.
If a child lives with ridicule, they learn to be shy.
If a child lives with shame, they learn to feel guilty.

If a child lives with tolerance, they learn to be patient.
If a child lives with encouragement, they learn confidence.
If a child lives with praise, they learn to appreciate.
If a child lives with fairness, they learn justice.
If a child lives with security, they learn to have faith.

If a child lives with approval, they learn to like themselves. If a child lives with acceptance and friendship, they learn to find love in the world!

THE GREAT NEWS

As a teenager or adult you can choose to change a behaviour at any time. And in turn let go of the negative beliefs that you've formed based on that old behaviour.

Our past doesn't have to dictate our future. In fact quite the opposite if we're willing to put in the effort.

So many celebrities have come from humble beginnings. And somehow managed to rise above their circumstances to become incredibly successful doing what they love. So if they can do it, so can you!

Jay-Z wasn't always the big music producer and rapper he is today. Before making it big, Jay-Z was living in the projects of Brooklyn, N.Y. Like most struggling families, his father left him at a young age and he was raised by his mother.

To make money and help his family, he resorted to selling drugs. He began rapping after his mother bought him a boom box and eventually uncovered his great talent. Today, he is one of the richest rappers in the world.

J.K. Rowling had a different life before the era of "Harry Potter." Before her famous stories began making millions, Rowling was living off welfare and trying to raise her child. It also didn't help that her mother passed away during this time of her life.

Her severe depression almost lead her to commit suicide, but writing saved her life. Today, she is the most successful author in the UK and has sold millions of of copies of her well-known series.

We would never think Justin Bieber came from a life of hardship. The singer is one of the biggest singing sensations since The Beatles. Little do people know, Bieber was born to a teen mom and used to live in a house that was infested with rats. He didn't have his own room or much of a bed, and food was low in the Bieber household.

He taught himself how to play different musical instruments and had no music training prior to becoming famous. Eventually he hit the fame scene when his YouTube videos were discovered.

Oprah Winfrey wasn't always the amazing talk show host. She was born in Mississippi, the daughter of a young teen. Oprah didn't even have enough money for clothes, so she wore dresses made out of potato sacks. She had a hard life dealing with sexual abuse from family and even became pregnant at the age of 14. She lost the baby shortly after and began to change her life around. She went to school and eventually her TV career began to go somewhere. Now she's a world wide household name and has one of the top television stations in the nation.

Jennifer Lopez may seem like she has all the money

and glamour now, but her life wasn't always so perfect. Her song, "Jenny from the Block" reveals some of the hardships and tough past Lopez went through. Lopez was born in Bronx, N.Y., which is one of the poorest towns of New York. She left home at a young age and lived in a dance studio. She juggled focusing on her career, taking dance lessons, and also working. Today, she is one of the biggest celebrities in multiple industries and holds the titles of singer, actress and fashion designer.

Leonardo Dicaprio can relate his own story to "The Great Gatsby." DiCaprio grew up in East Hollywood very poor. He was raised solely by his mother and was familiar with violence and drugs at a young age. His mother worked various jobs just to provide for her family. Leonardo's life started to take a turn for the better as a child after he started doing minor commercials. He eventually began doing TV shows and small movies. Today, he is a Golden Globe winner for Best Actor and we continue to see him in all the latest box-office hits.

Even though Jim Carrey is one of the biggest stars in movie comedies, he wasn't born with a silver spoon in his mouth. As a child, his father lost his job and this forced Carrey to work night shifts as a janitor. Carrey and his family lived out of their VW bus. After attending school he would then do an 8 hour shift working in a factory. Eventually he dropped out of school to look after this mother when she became sick.

He eventually made it big after performing in comedy shows at local nightclubs in Canada. He wanted to move into the film industry so he began taking supporting roles in as many movies as he could. He made his big break in "Ace Ventura: Pet Detective."

Hilary Swank lived most of her early life in a trailer park. Once her father left, it was up to her mother to raise her alone. The pair moved to Los Angeles so Swank could pursue acting.

EVERY DAY PEOPLE THAT HAVE NOT ALLOWED THEIR PAST TO DICTATE THEIR FUTURE

It would be remiss of me to just focus on celebrities that have risen above their circumstances. So many every day people (that are not house hold names) have also risen above their circumstances to live happy fulfilled lives. Some of them are my friends and I'm thrilled that they were willing to sharing their stories with you.

PETER'S STORY

I have always believed that almost anyone can achieve great things with self-belief and the support of good people. I was born in Hobart Australia in a mixed race family. My Australian mother was a clinically proven schizophrenic. She had many episodes and was a known local prostitute. My father was an underground criminal and drug dealer. They both abused drugs and were constantly involved in criminal activity. I spent my first 16 years being raised in one of the lowest socio economic housing commission suburbs where in the eighties and early nineties racism was at an all-time high. The local unemployment rate was seventy percent. Drug abuse, violence and mental health issues were a part of everyday life.

From ages sixteen to twenty six I lived in over twenty tiny apartments across as many cities. I followed in my parents footsteps with a disregard for the law. I owed 20k to the courts and had 20k of unsecured debt. The only person I loved, my grandfather died from cancer followed by my mother. I hit rock bottom and started abusing massive amounts of drugs daily. My one best friend had a severe accident that left him limbless and I didn't even visit him in hospital, nor did I call him to see if he was ok.

My friend didn't hold any grudges and called me one day asking if I was okay, and offered to support me to get my life back on track. He believed in me and trusted that one day I would succeed and achieve great things. We only spoke once a month as we lived 2000 kilometres away from each other, but having a mentor was what I needed to believe in myself.

I made a decision to get healthy both physically and mentally. I started working two jobs. In the daytime I was full-time as a sales rep and in the evenings I worked in a takeaway store. Within 3 years I managed to save a house deposit, get out of debt and achieve a good credit rating.

I soon fell in love and started a family with a beautiful partner, and not long afterwards we welcomed a healthy daughter. I worked even harder focusing on our future and finance, rather than enjoying my own family. My partner became bored with our repetitive lifestyle and found someone new. She left us both on a quest to travel the world and enjoy her life. So that now left me as a full-time single dad with a one year old daughter.

At that stage I had no choice but to involve myself in the community and ask for help from extended family, friends, clubs, groups and the government.

The love I had for my daughter made me realise that my parents must have loved me. So I forgave them. Extended family and community offered me assistance which resurrected my faith that there are many good people in the world. People really do care despite their criticism.

I felt so blessed to have their support, so decided it was only right for me to find a way to give back to my community.

Now age thirty four, I am a full-time single parent and full-time university student half way through my business degree. I have a brand new luxury apartment right in the

CBD. I contract manage the apartment block. I am an executive member of the community board and also on the committee of the local school. I am affiliated with charities and mentor many young adults, friends and single parents. My daughter is now four years old and is about to commence kindergarten at a local private school. We are both learning to read and write in another language so that one day we can live overseas.

KIM'S STORY

At the finale of a bankruptcy, losing my home and a divorce was where it I found it; my "rock bottom".

Feeling that I had no choices in life I later learned that I always have a choice. At this fork in the road, I could choose to bounce or die. With two young children I decided I needed to bounce. Funny thing about rock bottom, if you use it as a springboard it can launch you with some pretty good power.

I found myself on food stamps so that I could feed my kids and survive for the first four months. My Network Marketing business with Young Living Essential Oils had started to grow but was not yet something we could live off of. With my nose to the grind stone I continued to build and strangely enough I continued to grow on a personal level at the same time.

There were so many changes within the next couple

of years and many would comment on how fast I was moving. I guess a part of me realised it to a degree yet it felt good to make progress, it felt amazing to see the changes that were being created. Sometimes it was frightening beyond belief to step out there and do things on my own that I had never even imagined doing before. I was raised to get married, let your husband take care of you and your family, and be a good wife.

But what happens when things don't go as planned? No one had ever taught me how to handle life and take charge of my own life if I found myself in different circumstances than I had intended. So I continued leaning, growing and "bouncing". Each new milestone was like a breath of fresh air.

Four years after my bankruptcy I purchased our home on the river. It was beyond anything I thought we would live in and yet it has fit our family perfectly. Oh, family... Yes, I remarried. And I had another child. Business got bigger and better and more fulfilling with each new year. Along the way I found one of my main purposes in this life - to help other women realise or reclaim their power.

I've made friends I would never have met outside of my career. I bounced...plain and simple. And with each new level I enjoyed a certain high that I had never felt before. I've learned from so many over the years. The mentors have been wonderful. And now I enjoy mentoring others.

I blog about "Embracing Change and Creating a Healthy Lifestyle" at www.kimtheoilslady.com .

Through my online experience as well as my networking career I have met other women from all over the world and made some very wonderful friends. My years of lack, and my years of self doubt seem centuries ago. Yet I know they served a purpose. And if the only purpose was to equip me to help others out of their broken-ness and "stuck-ness" then it was all perfectly designed.

I believe every person has strength within them that they have hidden so deeply inside they may have no vision of it at this point. But it is there. I promise you...it is there.

HANEEF'S STORY

My story is of hardship, disappointment, anger and resentment. But it doesn't end that way. There truly was a light at the end of my tunnel.

My life changing experience happened to me at the tender age of eight. I remember being touched in my NoNo! Spot. As is often the case when children have been abused, I put the whole experience in the back of my mind, and pretended that it hadn't happened. I continued on with my life the best I could. At the same time being completely confused about what love from adults, and in particular the opposite sex looked like.

As I went about my life the best I could, it only got worse. To cut a long story short, my step dad moved in with us and became very abusive towards my mother. And when my mother was at work he hurled his abuse at me. If I said the wrong thing he would hit me with a closed fist. One time on the receiving end of his rage he knocked me out. When I came too he was towering over me with a look of joy on his face.

Did I just allow it to happen.? Gosh no. I fought back every time. So I was sent away to Oregon to stay with some close friends of my mothers. The lady she sent me to was suppose to be my Godmother. Little did my mum know that my godmother's husband was on drugs and on them bad. I won't go into details. Let's just say it changed me for the rest of my life.

When I finally came back to California things were okay for about three weeks. Then the hell began. I met my married thirty three year old step uncle who had a thing for little girls (such as myself.) I was fourteen going on fifteen when it began. He would tell my mother he was helping her out by taking me to school in the mornings. But that wasn't really what was happening. He was having sex with me first then dropping me at school. I was so confused. Confused about who I was, my worth, my emotions and so much more.

Somehow I managed to get through the whole ordeal. But at some point you have to crash and burn and deal with your truth. My breakdown happened at the age of thirty five. In my short life I had dealt with so much. And was now a wife, a mother, a student, and a career women. So I crashed. And I crashed hard.

I had to finally come to terms with the pain and humiliation of my past so that I could be free to love and enjoy my present and my future. My husband had to deal with a lot of rejection when it came to expressing his physical love toward me, but because of his love and understanding we were able to work through it together.

One of the biggest lessons I've learnt is to trust my intuition. Deep down I sensed what my uncle was doing was wrong. But at the time I didn't listen. And what I've learnt is that gentle voice inside of us is never wrong!

If you've been on the receiving end of any form of abuse; be it physical, mental or sexual abuse, I strongly encourage you to reach out and tell someone. Get the professional help you need to break the pattern for good, and free yourself of the shame and guilt. You do not deserve it. What you deserve is to lead a happy, fulfilled life.

I can now say I am in a great place. With a loving husband and two beautiful sons. I realised that my joy was a gift given by God. Something I was born with; and something no one could ever take away from me. I realised that happiness is a choice and a state of mind. So I choose to be happy and so I am.

I am the president of Not in my Home Foundation

www.nimhfoundation.com ~ a non profit organisation that provides self esteem classes to youth by giving them tools that will help them through out their lives. And I'm also the CEO of Touch my Closet.

LISA'S STORY

After the sudden and unexpected death of my mother, I became the caregiver and power of attorney for my father with Alzheimer's disease. All of his care, plus my already busy life, was overwhelming and emotionally devastating.

During this time, I learned more about myself than I had in the previous 30+ years combined. It forever changed my focus and direction. They say women are like tea bags, you never know how strong they are until you put them in hot water. Well, I had been simmering for a while. This experience illustrated how "going through" makes you stronger when you reach the other side...and that you can make it, IF you keep going.

My dad died 6 months to the day of my mother. I was alone by his side in the hospital when he passed. It had been a long and emotional journey. When I walked out of his hospital room that night, I walked out a different person.

I vowed to not waste the time I had left on this planet. Instead of drowning in sorrow, I decided to fully pursue my dreams, things people never thought I could accomplish.

With renewed determination, I finished the book I

had been working on and saw it through to completion. I chose to leave my "safe and steady" job in pursuit of more personal growth in a new field. From that launching point, I became a professional speaker set up my own business: www.getrealwellnesssolutions.com and even went back to school to further my degree.

I discovered that this tragedy was not a set back; it was a set up, to get me out of my comfort zone and into a life of purpose. Life is too short to live small. You are only guaranteed this moment, and now I strive to make the most of it.

THE POINT OF POWER IS RIGHT NOW

I'm so grateful to Peter, Kim, Haneef and Lisa for sharing their amazing stories. I hope you're realising by now that no matter what your early years were like, you can rise above them and create the life that you truly deserve?

Once you understand that you aren't your behaviours, and your beliefs were formed based on feedback you received about those behaviours and by copying your parents/care givers, you can re-connect with who you really are; what I refer to as your Unique Self.

And that in itself is usually a journey of self discovery. Think about how many years you've bought into the belief that you were flawed in some way? The great thing is that you are in a point of power right now to let go of those old limiting beliefs and behaviours.

CHAPTER FOUR

Develop Your Awareness

Sometimes we get so caught up doing our lives on "auto pilot" that we don't notice the clues along the way. Have you ever watched a butterfly navigate its way through your garden? It uses all of its senses to read the environment. Its antennae are checking for food, humans, obstacles etc.

As tiny children we did this. Some of us more so than others. However developing our awareness is a skill that we all need to develop as adults in order to learn, grown and develop to our true potential.

So in this chapter you'll get to create or fine tune your own set of antennae to guide you as you develop your awareness of who you are and who you can become.

He who knows other's is wise; he who knows himself is enlightened. ~ Lao Tzu

Part of defining self-confidence is thinking about what low self-confidence is, and what it looks and sounds like.

BECOME YOUR #1 FAN

Take this short quiz now.

Highlight or circle the statements that you think convey a lack of self-confidence.

1. "I may be wrong, but I think the answer is ten."
2. "Thank you for the compliment. I'm really proud of ...."
3. "That was really stupid of me."
4. "I forgot my assignment. I guess I left it at home."
5. (Responding to a compliment) "Oh, I've had this outfit for years."
6. "I would have gotten into the program, but they don't like to take people with my background."
7. "That sounds like a challenge. I'm sure we can figure out how to solve it, though."
8. "I'm sorry to interrupt, but I wonder if I could have a minute of your time."

Compare your answers to those listed below.

Answers to Quiz

Items 1, 3, 4, 5, 6, and 8 communicate low self-confidence. Of course, there are no 100% right answers, since many of the statements depend on context, tone of voice, cultural interpretation, and other factors. For example in the Asian culture showing extreme humility is a sign of confidence which could in other cultures be interpreted as shyness or a lack of confidence.

SIGNS OF SELF CONFIDENCE - QUIZ

Let's explore the meaning of self-confidence by taking a quiz. Read the list of statements below and check which ones, in your opinion, are signs of self-confidence.

1. Admitting when you are wrong.
2. Being flexible when change is needed.
3. Talking (versus boasting) about your accomplishments.

4. Describing negative events in positive terms. For example, "We didn't make our target, but we sure learned a lot."
5. Dressing to "fit in" and be accepted by your friends/colleagues/peers.
6. Using a strong handshake.
7. Using casual non specific language in an effort to avoid sounding too straight or serious. For example, "You guys did a cool thing."
8. Speaking very fast.
9. Smiling often.
10. Learning new skills.
11. Putting yourself down in order to sound humble.

Compare your answers

Answers to Quiz

Items 1, 2, 3, 4, 6, 9, and 10 are generally signs of self-confidence. The others could be seen as self-sabotaging behaviours.

SELF ASSESSMENT

Now it's time to focus specifically on you and how you feel about yourself.

ANSWER THE QUESTIONS BELOW TO ASSESS HOW CONFIDENT YOU FEEL AS A PERSON.

Usually the first response that comes to mind is the correct one, so have fun filling out the questionnaire. And remember that awareness is the first step to making positive changes in our lives. It's when we aren't aware that we just keep on repeating similar patterns over and over. Just like a mouse on a wheel running and running, using lots of energy, but getting nowhere.

Using a slide scale where 0 = Not at all, 5 = Sometimes, and 10 = Most of the time, answer the questions below.

1. I stand up for what I believe in, even if others disagree with me.
2. I feel confident in my work environment.

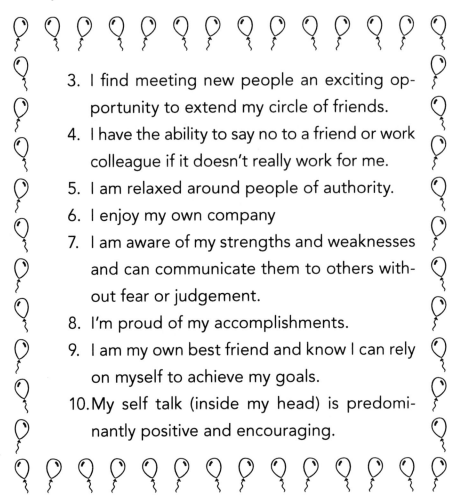

3. I find meeting new people an exciting opportunity to extend my circle of friends.
4. I have the ability to say no to a friend or work colleague if it doesn't really work for me.
5. I am relaxed around people of authority.
6. I enjoy my own company
7. I am aware of my strengths and weaknesses and can communicate them to others without fear or judgement.
8. I'm proud of my accomplishments.
9. I am my own best friend and know I can rely on myself to achieve my goals.
10. My self talk (inside my head) is predominantly positive and encouraging.

If you found this exercise confronting, please don't be disheartened by your answers. **Remember that Self-confidence is the result of a lot of hard work.** The process takes time. It has been said that **success is 99% persistence and 1% talent.** Congratulations on answering the questions. It shows your commitment to growing and learning.

The exciting thing is **it's never too late to get started on building your self confidence.** So take a moment and think of one thing that you could work on this week, that will assist you in taking baby steps towards feeling more confident about yourself?

CHAPTER FIVE

Break Free!

As a sixteen year old I proudly announced to my parents (and anyone else that would listen) that I was going to become a professional dancer. As a young child my dear friend Annie and I spent endless hours "dressing up" in my mums old ballroom dresses and petticoats and dancing up and down the corridors.

However I didn't attend my first formal dance class till the relatively late age of thirteen, when I chose Jazz Ballet for Sport. I remember coming home from my first class feeling so alive and elated that I'd found something that made my heart sing. Before long that one class a week became three and three became six. I loved everything about taking classes; the music, the costumes, the makeup, the performances, the lights and of course the applause!

Because I was the tallest in the class, I always got to be in the middle for our group performances , so I felt special. Added to that I got to do duos with the teacher's daughters, so I felt like a star. In hindsight I'm guessing I would have stood out like a sore thumb had my teacher put me anywhere else but the middle for the group numbers, however at the time I was none the wiser and felt ever so special. And I was a "big fish" in a little pond.

When I was sixteen years old and I announced my plans to become a professional dancer, my mum explained that I would need to expand my horizons and venture out into the big city studios and add ballet to my repertoire. Which I did.

I remember arriving at my first ballet class feeling nervous but incredibly excited. I proudly announced to the head of the school that I was going to become a dancer and that I knew I needed to take ballet classes. She eyed me up and down critically but agreed that I could take a beginner's class and then she would decide if I could continue after the class.

Well for anyone who's ever done a ballet class, you know that all the names of the movements are in French. So not only were all the movements new to me, I hadn't a clue what the teacher was saying. So I just did my best to mimic the students closest to me. And I thought I'd done a pretty good job, all things considered.

But alas, when the teacher called me into her office after the class she said something like: "let's face it dear, you're really not built for ballet you're,

- Too tall
- Too old
- Have flat feet (instead of the ideal high insteps)
- Turned in hips (again a big no no)
- So you might as well forget it!

Can you imagine how devastated I was? What did she mean "forget it?" I was going to be a dancer. I knew I had a dancer inside. Why couldn't she see it? I had no desire to be a ballerina, but I knew if I was going to become a professional dancer that I needed a strong ballet foundation.

I remember my mother picking me up after the class and sobbing my heart out all the way home as I told her what had happened. After I'd calmed down and run out of tears, my mother suggested we try another school. So off I went to another big school in the city with my big dream of becoming a professional dancer, only to be told the same thing.

Again, my mother said, "You just haven't found the right school yet, let's try another one." So once again I ventured out for the third time only to be told the same thing: "I might as well forget it!"

I remember having a family discussion and my dad saying, "Well you have two choices. You can listen to your critics or you can prove them wrong."

He'd been an Australian Cycling Champion and his speciality had been sprinting. However when his mates had teased him and told him he was only built for speed and not long distance, he went out and proved them wrong by winning a road race. So I had a great teacher.

I decided to take his advice and kept searching until I eventually found a school that focused on my strengths, and lovingly developed my weaknesses.

The name of the school was Bodenweisers (named after one of the pioneers of modern dance Gertrude Bodenweiser). Margaret Chapple or "Chappie" as we fondly called her had been Gertrude's Protege. Chappie never once made me feel inadequate or second rate. Instead she encouraged me to be the best dancer I could be.

But in all honesty I had given up on my dream of becoming a professional dancer and only took classes for my own pleasure.

When I was twenty one I travelled overseas to join my English boyfriend who had been in Australia on a working holiday. However, as fate would have it, on the exact day I flew into Heathrow Airport in London he flew off to the US to be a Trek America Tour Guide for 6 months.

So after touring around England, Scotland and Wales with a friend I decided if I was in London I might as well take some dance classes. I looked in the Yellow Pages Phone Directory for schools and found one quite close by called "Una Billings TV School of Dance in Hammersmith." Little did I know that my life was about to change dramatically. I attended a few casual classes and before I knew it I was studying full time with wonderful teachers who believed in me. Especially in my weakest style of dance, Ballet.

I began to blossom under the watchful and incredibly encouraging eye of Fernand Monet. He was the Ballet Master for the Royal Ballet when they went on tour. But when the company wasn't touring we got to take classes with him. And what a gift he was! Instead of making me feel inadequate he used to say incredibly encouraging things like, "developé those million dollar legs right up to the sky Kathy, extra inch, extra hundred pounds a week."

I knew I had a lot of catching up to do, and I finally had people that believed in me. So I immersed myself. On my days off you'd find me rolling a drink bottle forward and back to strengthen my instep, stretching to improve my flexibility, using the bathroom sink as my ballet barre, practising all of my routines and pirouetting, jumping and leaping my way all around my tiny apartment.

Six months later Una (the head of the school) informed me I was ready to start auditioning for jobs. Much to my delight, when I started auditioning for jobs, I realised my height turned out to be my biggest asset! Yes you read correctly! My height turned out to be my biggest asset. There were only about 50 dancers at a Tall Girl Audition versus 200+ for the general auditions, so the odds were stacked in my favour.

Finally I was able to "Break Free" of the negative boxes and labels that those first few ballet teachers had put me in and become the professional dancer that I'd dreamt of for so many years.

What I learnt from that whole experience is summed up beautifully in a song by Jana Stanfield called "Let your life lead you where you need to go."

Here are the lyrics:

> *Every once in a while I start losing my smile and I say to myself what's the deal? What exactly's the point, getting all out of joint? Not liking the way that I feel? Maybe I believe that its all up to me, at the helm of this boat all alone. Till some stormy detail, takes the wind from my sail to remind me what I've always known. Relax and let the river flow, let your life teach you what you need to know, let your life lead you where you need to go. Let your life teach you what you need to know, let your life lead you where you need to go.*

Unfortunately, I'm not the only one that has been put in a negative box or label.

CELEBRITIES THAT HAVE BROKEN FREE OF THEIR NEGATIVE BOXES AND LABELS

Did you know?

- A Baltimore TV producer told Oprah that she was "unfit for television news." Evening news reporter Oprah Winfrey couldn't help but get emotionally invested in her stories. The producer of Baltimore's WJZ-TV got fed up and pulled her off the air. As a consolation, he offered her a role on a daytime TV show. Winfrey was initially heartbroken. At the time, daytime TV was a huge step down from the evening news. Her sadness quickly faded as the show, "People Are Talking", became a hit. That success helped Oprah find her true calling as a talk show host.

- Barbra Streisand's mother told her to forget acting and become a school secretary like she was? Thankfully she didn't.

- Michael Jordan was cut from his High School Basketball Team and look what he went on to do!

- The Beatles were told, "guitar groups are on the way out." And a well known record label said, "The

Beatles are on their way out." After that The Beatles signed with EMI and they brought Beatlemania to the United States and became the greatest band in history.

- Stephanie Meyer, the author of the *Twilight* Series sent 15 letters to literary agencies. Five didn't reply, nine rejected. One gave her a chance and then eventually eight publishers auctioned for the right to publish *Twilight*. She got a three book deal worth $750,000.00. In 2010 *Forbes* reported that she earned $40 million.

- Steven Spielberg applied and was denied two times to the prestigious University of California film school. Instead he went to Cal State University in Long beach. He went on to direct some of the biggest movie blockbusters in history. Now he's worth $2.7 billion and ironically in 1994 got an Honorary Degree from the film school that rejected him twice.

- In 1919, Walt Disney was fired from the Kansas City Star. According to his editor, he "lacked imagination and had no good ideas." That wasn't the last of his failures. Disney then acquired Laugh-O-Gram, an animation studio he later drove into bankruptcy. Finally, he decided to set his sights on a more profitable area: Hollywood. He and his brother moved to California and started producing a successful cartoon series. Legend has it he was turned down 302 times before he got financing for creating Disneyland.

- Albert Einstein didn't speak till he was four and didn't read till seven. His parents and teachers thought he was mentally handicapped. He won a Nobel Prize and became the face of Modern Physics.

- Colonel Sanders started his dream at age 65. He got a Social Security Check for only $105 and was mad. Instead of complaining he did something about it. He thought restaurant owners would love his fried chicken recipe, use it, their sales would increase and he'd get a percentage of it. He drove around the country knocking on doors, sleeping in his car and wearing his white suit. Do you know how many times people said no? A whopping 1009 times.

- J.K Rowling, the author of Harry Potter, spoke to the Graduating Class of Harvard in June 2008. She didn't talk about success. She talked about failures. Her own in particular. I absolutely love her quote. "You might never fail on the scale I did," Rowling told that privileged audience. "But it is impossible to live without failing at something, unless you live so cautiously that you might as well not have lived at all—in which case, you fail by default." She should know. The author didn't magically become richer than the Queen of England overnight. Penniless, recently divorced, and raising a child on her own, she wrote the first Harry Potter book on an old manual typewriter. 12 publishers rejected the manuscript! A year later she was given the green light by Barry Cunningham from Bloomsbury, who agreed to publish the book but insisted she get a day job because there was no money in children's books. What if she stopped at the first rejection? The fifth? Or the tenth?

The measure of success can be shown by how many times someone keeps going despite hearing only "no".

So what boxes and labels have you been put in? And what have you been told you'll never achieve? By society, your parents, your teachers, your siblings, your friends and even yourself???

Whether they're positive or negative boxes, chances are they've either restricted you or put massive pressure on you to live up to them. Isn't it time to break free?

Its time for you to break on through. Get un-stuck, and do that thing you've been aching to do. ~ Oprah Winfrey

BECOME YOUR #1 FAN

You'll need a blank piece of paper (not your journal), a pen, a garbage bin, a wash basin, hand soap, a towel and some music: I suggest "Another one Bites the Dust" by Queen. And your favourite uplifting piece of music. Some suggestions: "Roar" by Katy Perry, "I've got the Power" by Snap, The Theme from Rocky, "Eye of the Tiger", "I am Woman". Whatever you choose make sure it puts you in an energised, uplifted state.

Here are links to the songs I mentioned on You Tube.

MUSIC TO RIP UP YOUR PAPER TO:

ANOTHER ONE BITES THE DUST by Queen
http://www.youtube.com/watch?v=Wz_DNrKVrQ8

POWER MUSIC TO CELEBRATE AFTERWARDS

ROAR by Katy Perry
http://www.youtube.com/watch?v=CevxZvSJLk8
THE POWER by Snap
http://www.youtube.com/watch?v=vUb_S4e-Rd4
THE THEME FROM ROCKY
http://www.youtube.com/watch?v=ioE_O7Lm0I4
EYE OF THE TIGER
http://www.youtube.com/watch?v=btPJPFnesV4
I AM WOMAN
http://www.youtube.com/watch?v=lWDLDPIFBFQ

Once you've chosen your song you can move on to the exercise below:

Take a moment now and think about the boxes and labels that you've been put in?

While playing "Another one bites the dust" (or any music you feel represents letting go of something that no longer serves you) get out a pen and blank piece of loose paper (not your journal) and write down all the negative things that people (including yourself) have told you about yourself. For example, you're lazy, your ugly, you're stupid, you're dumb, you'll never achieve, you're a loser etc.

Give yourself the time and space to do this and I bet you'll be surprised and relieved to get them out of your head and heart and onto paper.

Once you've done that, scribble all over your paper in big red letters NOT TRUE!

Crank up the volume as you rip the paper to shreds, and either burn it or put it in the garbage where it belongs!

Then go and wash your hands and visualise releasing all of those negative emotions as they make their way down the drain.

Immediately after that put on some uplifting music that makes you feel powerful (either from my suggestions or one of your own.) Sing, dance and enjoy the oh so wonderful emotions that come from finally letting those suckers go.

Stand in a Powerful Pose (I suggest you make two fists and raise your arms in the air) and announce to yourself and the world, that you are re-claiming who you really are! (This is called

Anchoring and you'll learn more about it in future chapters.)

Then with your music playing in the background write in your journal how doing that exercise made you feel?

The exercise above is a great way to start the process of weeding all the negative thoughts and beliefs from your emotional garden. In order to become your #1 Fan you need to look after your emotional garden with loving care; pull out the weeds, fertilise your soil, plant new seeds everyday, water them and watch them blossom and grow!

CHAPTER SIX

Silence Your Inner Critic

I love the quote below by Vincent Van Gogh. Talk about being way ahead of his time? The word Neuroplasticity didn't even exist when he was alive, however Van Gogh knew how to silence his inner critic. And you can too!

> *If you hear a voice inside you saying you're not a painter, then by all means paint and that voice will be silenced. ~ Vincent Van Gogh*

THE PLASTICITY OF THE HUMAN BRAIN

A landmark 1998 human study found that the human brain has the ability to develop new brain cells. Prior to that it was believed that the adult brain was fixed and unchanging. It was long believed that once we grow up, our brains have a set number of neurones performing functions in a fixed way.

The truth is that we are continuously changing although we may not always realise it. For example, most of the cells and tissues in the human body keep regenerating and are much younger than the person in which they are found. You may have heard a statement that our body changes every seven years. The average age depends on the types of cells and tissues, some take much less time to renew, others take longer. Your habits and your lifestyle all have an impact on how your body turns out.

Neuroscientists tell us now that our brain can also rejuvenate and improve itself. Our brain forms new neurones throughout our lives, and the connections and functions in the brain change as well. What we do day to day influences our brain's function, and we can participate actively and consciously in the rewiring of our brain. The brain's ability to rewire itself as a result of life experiences is called Neuroplasticity. That's right, our brains are plastic.

Norman Doidge in his book, The Brain that Changes Itself: Stories of Personal Triumph from the Frontiers of Brain Science, talks about a paradox of change. The forces that enable us to change are also responsible for keeping us stuck. If we keep doing the same, we may think nothing changes, but in fact, the more we repeat a certain behaviour, the stronger the corresponding pathway in the brain grows, making it more difficult to unlearn the pattern. The good news is that the same principle applies when we learn a new skill or habit. The more attention we pay to it and the more we practice it, the easier it will become.

As you read the following remarkable examples of Neuroplasticity in action, consider how much power you actually have to shape your brain and your life. It's never too late to change and build new good habits.

- The adult human brain has approximately 100 billion neurones. Education increases the number of branches among neurones, increasing the volume and thickness of the brain. Our brain is like a muscle that needs mental work-outs. Learning and brain exercises slow age-related mental decline and even improve brain function.

- Physical exercise promotes creation of new neurones in the brain, the process known as neurogenesis. It also stimulates sensory and motor cortices and helps the brain's balance system.

- Specifically designed brain exercises have been shown to strengthen weak brain functions in children and adults with learning disabilities. For example, rote memorisation can help the auditory memory. Handwriting strengthens motor capacities, and adds speed and fluency to reading.

- Stroke patients recover some lost abilities when the brain reorganises itself to move functions from the damaged location to a new one.

- Because the brain physically changes its state as we think, it is possible to measure the changes electronically. As a result, there's technology that allows completely paralysed people to move objects with their thoughts and interact with computers.

- V.S. Ramachandran, Director of the Centre for Brain and Cognition and Professor with the Psychology Department and Neurosciences Program at the University of California, San Diego, uses imagination and illusion to restructure brain maps and help people manage their phantom pain and some forms of chronic pain, which he believes to be a construct of the brain that is projected on to the body. For example, his invention of the mirror box helped many amputees get rid of the pain in the phantom limb. The brain is tricked into believing that the phantom limb is moving when the patient sees a mirror reflection of the moving good limb in the mirror box.

- People can improve performance through visualisations because action and imagination often activate the same parts of the brain. When we need to learn a physical skill, mental practice of this skill can produce the same physical changes in the motor system as the physical practice. This effect has been achieved in experiments that involved people learning to play the piano, as well as athletes in training.

- If you were to wear blindfolds for two days, your visual cortex would reorganise itself to process sound and touch. Once you take the blindfolds off, the visual cortex will stop responding to tactile or auditory signals within twelve or twenty-four hours.

- The Sea Gypsies, Nomadic people who live in a cluster of tropical islands in the Burmese archipelago and spend most of their lives in boats on the open sea, can see clearly under water at great depths because they learn to control the shape of their lenses and the side of their pupils, constricting them 22%. Most of us can't do that, and pupil adjustment has been considered to be affixed, innate reflex. However, in one study, Swedish children were able to learn the trick, and their brains responded to the training.

- Collaboration between Richard Davidson, a neuroscientist at the University of Wisconsin-Madison and the Dalai Lama explored the effects of meditation on the brain. The researchers compared the trained minds of the monks and those of the volunteers. The results showed much greater activation of powerful gamma waves in the monks than in the students during meditation. Moreover, even when the participants were not meditating, the trained meditators' brains showed a large increase in the gamma signal. In previous studies, mental activities such as focus, memory, learning and consciousness were associated with the kind of enhanced neural coordination found in the meditators. The intense gamma waves signalled higher mental activity and heightened awareness.

- Learning to juggle can increase grey matter in the occipital-temporal cortex as early as after 7 days of training.

By now I hope you are starting to realise that you're in control of your brain and not vice versa?

If you are like most of the population, you probably have some negative self talk going on inside your head? That nagging voice that puts you down, and tells you that you aren't good enough, clever enough, pretty or handsome enough, fit enough, financially savvy enough, successful enough etc. **Most of us have a bottom line belief of "I'm not good enough".**

That voice can have a devastating effect on how we feel about ourselves. There are lots of tools to assist you in quieting that negative voice, and then replacing it with a positive, encouraging voice. It takes practice, but hey what have you got to lose? Just the critical voice that puts you down!

If you have access to the internet you can watch a video on my website that walks you through how to Create your own Personal Cheer Squad. Click on the link below:

http://theconfidencecoach.net.au/resources_videos.html

If you have a Smart Phone you can scan the code below:

Or if you prefer you can just keep reading and I'll explain how to do it.

HOW TO RE-PROGRAM YOUR NEGATIVE
SELF TALK

There are four ways you can re-program your negative self talk. I encourage you to try all four and then decide what works best for you.

1. Drown it out. Some people have great success telling the voice "out of here, I don't need you any more."
2. Change the volume. Imagine you have a remote control and either hit the mute button or turn the volume right down.
3. Change the tone of the voice inside your head. You've probably spent many years perfecting the negative voice, so instead of changing what you're saying, it's usually easier to try changing the emotion behind the words. For example if you say something like "you silly idiot", try saying it now in a Donald Duck or goofy type of voice. Take a moment now to experiment. Does it take away the negative impact? It might even make you feel like laughing because it sounds so hilarious. The other thing you might like to try, is to change the tone to a very sexy sultry voice. What affect does that have on you?

4. Change the negative comment to a positive comment. Because your critical voice has probably had years of practice its usually easier to add a positive onto the end of a negative. There are three magical words that can transform a negative statement into a positive one. I've come up with an acronym to help you remember them. I call them a Y.U.I. Just like when we do a U turn in a car it takes us in a totally different direction, adding one of the phrases below will totally change the way you feel about yourself.

Y. = YET
U. = UP UNTIL NOW
I. = IN THE PAST

For example:

~ "I can't reprogram my negative self talk "yet." By adding one tiny word to the end of your sentence it implies that you will be able to do it if you stay focused and persistent.
~ "My negative self talk has stopped me from applying for that promotion up until now" This phrase creates the impetus in your brain to create a different outcome.

~ "In the past, I used to let my negative self talk hold me back." By simply adding in the past to the beginning of the sentence it puts your limiting beliefs back in the past where they belong, and sets you free to create a new outcome.

Changing the voice inside your head takes consistent effort but speaking from personal experience, it is very liberating when at last the negative voice is replaced with one that is supportive, encouraging and on your side!

Neuro Scientist's have proven that Neurones in our brain that fire together, wire together.

Here's a picture of the Dendrites in our brains making new connections.

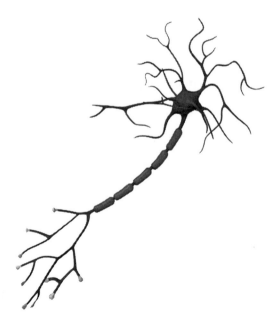

The key to rewiring new neural pathways is consistency. So be persistent. Every time your negative self talk rears its ugly head, use the skills you just learnt to reprogram it. And over time you'll create your own internal cheer squad!

WHAT IS N.L.P. or NEURO LINGUISTIC PROGRAMMING?

Neurolinguistic programming is concerned with the patterns or programming created by the interactions among the brain, language, and the body, that produce both effective and ineffective behaviour. The founders of NLP were John Grinder a linguistic professor and Richard Bandler a mathematician, at the University of California at Santa Cruz (UCSC), around 1975.

ANCHORING

In the field of NLP there's a term called anchoring. Anchoring is a process by which a stimulus triggers a response/state.

Our minds naturally link experiences as a way of giving meaning to them. Through our history many states/experiences become linked/associated with a different stimuli.

Emotional states have a powerful and pervasive

influence on our thinking and behaviours. Sometimes, unknowingly we've anchored states in ways that can be very limiting and detrimental. Other anchoring can be very useful; conserving resources and being positive and supportive in many ways.

If you watch most elite level athletes they've either been trained to use anchoring or do it instinctually every time they have a win.

HOW TO SET UP A POSITIVE ANCHOR

Every time you have a win reprogramming your critical voice - whether its a small, medium or big win...... celebrate like crazy! Do a celebration dance, blow up a balloon, or if you're out in public find a way to celebrate that works for the environment you're in. Say yes and make a fist or something similar. As I mentioned before, we're all anchoring in positive and negative experiences throughout our day without even knowing it, so take control and make sure that you say something positive, either in your head or out loud, and do something subtle or big with your body at the same time. The key is consistency; every time you have a win, anchor it in. It's called stacking anchors, and basically what you are doing is building a solid foundation of success in your body so that you can set off your positive anchors whenever you want to feel successful.

I do it all the time. I have my "power move" that I do every time I have a personal win. I curl my fingers on both hands into fists, take my arms out in front of me at waist height and then pull them in to either side of my hips as I let out a very loud celebratory "YES!!!" If I'm out in public and it's not appropriate I still make my fists, and say yes inside my head!

Just before I'm going to do something that takes me out of my "comfort zone" I set off my positive anchor by doing my power move. My pulse changes, my eyes become focused, my breathing changes and positive emotions surge through every cell in my body. And then I proceed to do whatever I want to do in a state of confidence, joy, curiosity and positive anticipation! And in that state everything I do, I do better!

So have fun anchoring in your wins and setting them off when you need them.

CHAPTER SEVEN

Who Are You Really?

Ultimately we all need to be loved, wanted and appreciated. Unfortunately in the process of getting those needs met, we often sell ourselves out. And become who we think everyone else wants us to be. And in that process lose touch with who we really are.

In Chapter Three you discovered that you are not your behaviours. You learnt those from everyone around you in order to fit in. So you may be wondering "well if I'm not my behaviours then who am I?" And that's a great question to be asking yourself.

> *Who am I anyway? Am I my resumé that is a*
> *picture of a person I don't know? What does*
> *he want from me? What should I try to be?*
> *All these face all around and here we go.*
> *~ Lyrics from Chorus Line the Musical.*

When I decided to live (after I'd reached rock bottom) I spent a lot of time analysing myself and my behaviours. Prior to that I had always kept myself too busy out there in the world to really stop and question who I was.

I asked myself lots of questions like:

- Why do I teach dance?
- Do I do it because I love it?
- Do I do it because I'm good at it?
- Do I do it because I've done it a long time and it's comfortable?
- Do I do it because everyone else (especially my parents) expect me to keep doing it?

I also asked myself tough questions like:

- Which behaviours have I learnt from my mother, that don't really serve me?
- Which behaviours have I learnt from my father, that don't really serve me?
- What beliefs have I formed about relationships based on how my mother and father interact with each other?
- What have I taken on board from my parents, that has nothing to do with me? i.e., their feelings of not being good enough, their disappointment in not having a fulfilling marriage etc.

- What did I learn about money, sex, relationships, being successful?

Along with that I also focused on the positive questions too, like:

- What positive traits have I learnt from my parents?
- What behaviours have I learnt from my parents that are positive and empowering?
- What am I grateful for?
- What's the best way to show my gratitude?

Asking yourself these sorts of questions is a great way to get to know yourself better. And be patient with yourself. The answers may not come straight away. But just by putting your focus on them, as you do your day, you'll build your awareness and in turn get your answers.

A word of warning, if this is the first time you've done this type of thing its quite normal to feel a bit uncomfortable doing this. Sometimes people feel like they're being disloyal to their parents by analysing their negative behaviours and beliefs. If this is the case for you, I recommend you acknowledge you're feelings and do the exercise anyway. As that well known saying goes "The truth will set you free."

So let's get started.

BECOME YOUR #1 FAN

I call this exercise a Behaviours and Beliefs Audit.

Get out your journal and on the top of one page write POSITIVE and on the top of another page write NEGATIVE.

ON THE POSITIVE PAGE ASK YOURSELF THESE QUESTIONS:

~ What positive traits have I learnt from my mother/female caregiver?

~ What positive traits have I learnt from my father/male caregiver?

~ What behaviours and beliefs have I learnt from my mother/caregiver that are positive and empowering?

~ What behaviours and beliefs have I learnt from my father/caregiver that are positive and empowering?

ON THE NEGATIVE PAGE ASK YOURSELF THESE QUESTIONS:

~ Which traits have I learnt from my mother/caregiver, that don't really serve me?

~ Which traits have I learnt from my father/caregiver, that don't really serve me?

~ Which behaviours have I learnt from my mother/caregiver, that don't really serve me?

~ Which behaviours have I learnt from my father/caregiver, that don't really serve me?

~ Which beliefs have I learnt from my mother/caregiver, that don't really serve me?

~ Which beliefs have I learnt from my father/caregiver, that don't really serve me?

~ What beliefs have I formed about relationships based on how my mother and father interact/ed with each other?

ON A FRESH PAGE ASK YOURSELF:
What beliefs did I unconsciously take on board from my parents/caregivers about:

~ money (creating it, managing it, deserving it etc....)

~ sex

~ health

~ food

~ relationships

~ being successful

~ leading a happy fulfilling life

~ deserving to be financially prosperous

Developing your awareness is the first step to being able to change aspects of who you are. Until you're aware of a particular behaviour or belief you can't do anything about changing it.

I discovered all sorts of things about myself when I did this exercise, that I had never stopped to notice.

For instance, I realised that I had taken on board my mother's nervous energy around getting to where I was going on time. Most of the time mum was "running late" and I had unconsciously replicated that. To this day, sometimes I have to stop myself and take a few deep breaths and remind myself that this behaviour isn't who I am. I learnt it from my mum, so I remind myself to relax, breathe deeply and trust that I'll arrive at the perfect time. And inevitably I do. If I am running late it usually turns out that the other person is too!

The environment we grow up in has a huge impact on how we feel about ourselves and our place in the world.

I remember looking in the mirror years ago and realising that I had a frown line in exactly the same place as my mum. Now did I ever say to myself "I want to be like my mum, so I'll create a frown line in exactly the same place as her?" Of course not, it happened unconsciously.

I can hear some of you saying, yeah well that's just genetic, but I was adopted, so that blows that theory out of the water.

It's nothing to do with genes, its about us being

sponges as children, and unconsciously soaking up the good and the not so good stuff from our environment.

As I mentioned earlier, awareness is a great thing. Once we're aware, we can choose to either discard or continue with an attitude, belief, or behaviour.

RECLAIMING YOUR TRUE SELF

Underneath your "persona" is your true self. We all wear masks to varying degrees. The more comfortable we are in our own skin, the more willing we are to show the world who we really are. The less comfortable the larger the "act" or "persona."

I recently studied with a woman called Jean Haner. She's a Hay House Author and runs a course called *The Wisdom of your Face*. I've always been fascinated by what drew me to one person and repelled me from another. And known that a lot of that was what I was unconsciously picking up from their face and body language.

For years I've noticed that lots of people (including celebrities) often have one eye larger and more open than the other. And what I learnt in Jean's course was that it has to do with how comfortable we are at showing all aspects of who we are to the world around us.

You see, our left eye represents our private self; how we feel about ourselves when no one is watching. Our right eye represents our public face; what we show the world. Often people will wear their "mask/persona" in public but in the comfort of their own home feel entirely different. So if there's a discrepancy between the two, it shows up in our eyes and other facial features.

It's fascinating. And the more comfortable we feel in our skin, the more even our features become.

RE-CONNECT WITH YOUR INNER CHILD

As we grow up and become adults we feel we have to act mature and in the process often lose sight of the fact that we still have a little child inside of us that wishes that we would acknowledge her/him from time to time. So let's get started reconnecting with your Inner Child that resides in your adult body.

You may not even now they exist as there are probably years of conditioning, that has forced you to push them into the background. But just like the baggage carousel at the airport with a lone piece of luggage waiting for someone to claim it, your little child that lives inside your adult body has been waiting patiently for you to come back and collect her/him.

BECOME YOUR #1 FAN

You'll need a picture of yourself as a tiny baby aged 0-18 months. If for any reason you can't find a picture of yourself, look for one in a magazine or online that represents how you think you would have looked back then.

Reclaim your true self now:

- Look into your tiny baby's eyes

- While you continue looking into her/his eyes, ask them to forgive you for unknowingly abandoning them.

- Re-assure them that from this moment on you will love them and treat them with the love and respect that they truly deserve.

- Commit to being there for your inner child, starting today!

Its quite normal to experience tears as you do this exercise. Just allow the tears to flow knowing that deep healing is occurring.

- Make three copies of your picture and put one up in your bedroom, another one in your bathroom, and carry one on your phone or in your wallet as a constant reminder to treat yourself with the love and respect you deserve.

- Every morning on waking look into your tiny chid's eyes and tell them that you're there for them.

- Find your own unique ways to remind yourself everyday to be there for your inner child.

- Ask your Inner Child what you can do to nurture them. And listen for the answers (as absurd as they might sound to your adult self.) Perhaps they'd like to sing? Or to dance? Or make paper airplanes? Or jump in puddles? Or roll down a grass hill? When we become adults we often become way too serious for our own good. If the idea of doing something child like horrifies you, I encourage you to to take a deep breath and become comfortable being uncomfortable at first. Over time your adult self will enjoy interacting with your Inner Child.

- Doing things that are playful connects us with our spirit and makes our hearts sing.

- Reconnect with your Inner Child every day and respect their hopes, dreams and desires (no matter how silly you may feel at first) and in turn watch your self esteem and self worth blossom.

Years ago I created a poster that had a picture of me as a baby as well as a recent picture of me as an adult. And the heading said, "It's time to RECLAIM YOUR MAGNIFICENCE." Every morning I started my day looking into my tiny child's eyes and committed to being there for her.

Even now, each day, I look for ways to allow my inner child to come out and play. Have you heard the saying "It's never too late to have a happy childhood?" There were aspects of my childhood that brought me happiness, but there were also plenty of situations (many beyond my control) that robbed me of some of my joy and sense of security. While I can't go back and change what happened, I can make sure that I seize every opportunity to create joy in my life today! And so can you.

And life will present you with wonderful opportunities to do so.

One day, it had been raining and my daughter (who was about 6 at the time) and I were walking home from school. We lived in a small country town and our 15 minute walk home included walking on a red dirt road and you guessed it, there were lots of pot holes. The first time she jumped into a puddle I caught myself saying "Don't do that". But as the words escaped from my mouth, I looked down at my beautiful little girl and saw the expression of sheer joy written all over her face. And that was enough for me to recognise that this was a magical moment and an opportunity for me to loosen up and live a little! So what did we do? We jumped in every single puddle we could find and arrived home, soaked to the skin, totally saturated in red mud, and giggling like a couple of 3 year olds that had been up to no good!

We then proceeded to have hot baths and showers.

And let's face it, all the clothes needed was a good soak too and they were as good as new again. And we had created a magical moment that I know both of us will treasure forever!

A few years later I went to pick my daughter up from her new school in the city, and unexpectedly the heavens opened up and it began to pour with rain. I'm not talking about a passing shower, it was bucketing down. And you guessed it, no raincoats or umbrellas in sight. We both saw a child and their mother running past bare foot with their shoes in their hands. My daughter and I looked at each other and without saying a word, we both took off our shoes and ran out into the rain to look for puddles!

I treasure those magical moments and I hope that when my daughter grows up she remembers to do the same with her children!

So **what could you do today that lights up your inner child?** Might it be something as simple as wearing clothes in your favourite colour? Or dancing to your favourite music. Or doing some finger painting? Blowing bubbles? Making mud pies? Or writing a poem? Flying a kite? Sitting in a hammock and watching the world go by? Whatever it is I encourage you to do it, even if you feel a little silly at first!

BECOME YOUR #1 FAN

If you haven't done so already, its time to create your Become your #1 Fan Journal. It could be a textbook or hard cover notebook. Spend time making it unique like you. You might like to put a photo of yourself as a baby and one of you now on the cover or front page? Or perhaps cover it in your favourite colours, or pictures, or make a collage of your favourite positive affirmations. Do whatever works for you and spend time at least once a week writing down your feelings. Taking the time to really connect with how you are feeling or have felt through the week is a great way to develop confidence in your ability to be there for yourself.

Track your wins no matter how small. It's also a great place to write down your dreams and desires. What do you dream of doing/being/having? What would you do if you knew you couldn't fail?

One of my favourite sayings is "If it's to be, it's up to me!" You see no one else can really change how you feel about yourself. Just like Michael Jackson's song "Man in the Mirror" ~ If you want to change any aspect of your behaviours, beliefs or attitudes it's ultimately up to you!

CHAPTER EIGHT

Who's in the Driver's Seat?

Would you agree that when we get behind the wheel of a car, it's ultimately up to us where we end up? If we have a clear idea of where we're headed we're far more likely to get to our destination than if we just get behind the wheel and drive aimlessly around. If we know where we want to end up but don't have a GPS we might get lost, but eventually if we keep asking for directions we'll eventually get to our destination.

In life, lots of people do their lives on automatic pilot allowing fear to dictate what they do and don't do. They don't realise that by making a few adjustments they can take control of their lives. The key is in staying persistent and not allowing fear to take over.

According to a blog on Psychology Today: Fear is a vital response to physical and emotional danger—if we didn't feel it, we couldn't protect ourselves from legitimate threats. But often we fear situations that are

89

far from life-or-death, and thus hang back for no good reason. Traumas or bad experiences can trigger a fear response within us that is hard to quell. Yet exposing ourselves to our personal demons is the best way to move past them.

A simple and useful definition of fear is:

An anxious feeling, caused by our anticipation of some imagined event or experience.

Medical experts tell us that the anxious feeling we get when we're afraid is a standardised biological reaction. It's pretty much the same set of body signals, whether we're afraid of getting bitten by a dog, getting turned down for a date, or getting our taxes audited.

Fear, like all other emotions, is basically information. It offers us knowledge and understanding, if we choose to accept it, of our psychobiological status.

Here is some fascinating information about Fear from Dr. Karl Albrecht Author, *Practical Intelligence ~ the Art and Science of Common Sense.*

There are only five basic fears, out of which almost all of our other so-called fears are manufactured. Those five basic fears are:

- Extinction - fear of annihilation, of ceasing to exist. This is a more fundamental way to express it than just calling it the "fear of death". The idea of no longer being arouses a primary existential anxiety in all normal humans. Consider that panicky feeling you get when you look over the edge of a high building.

- Mutilation - fear of losing any part of our precious bodily structure; the thought of having our body's boundaries invaded, or of losing the integrity of any organ, body part, or natural function. For example, anxiety about animals, such as bugs, spiders, snakes, and other creepy things arises from fear of mutilation.

- Loss of Autonomy - fear of being immobilised, paralysed, restricted, enveloped, overwhelmed, entrapped, imprisoned, smothered, or controlled by circumstances. In a physical form, it's sometimes known as claustrophobia, but it also extends to social interactions and relationships.

- Separation - fear of abandonment, rejection, and loss of connectedness - of becoming a non-person - not wanted, respected, or valued by anyone else. The "silent treatment," when imposed by a group, can have a devastating psychological effect on the targeted person.

- Ego-death - fear of humiliation, shame, or any other mechanism of profound self-disapproval that threatens the loss of integrity of the Self; fear of the shattering or disintegration of one's constructed sense of lovability, capability, and worthiness.

That's all - just those five.

Think about the various common labels we put on our fears. Start with the easy ones:

- Fear of heights or falling is basically fear of extinction (possibly accompanied by significant mutilation, but that's sort of secondary).
- Fear of failure? Read it as fear of ego-death.
- Fear of rejection? It's fear of separation, and probably also fear of ego-death. The terror many people have at the idea of having to speak in public is basically fear of ego-death.
- Fear of intimacy, or "fear of commitment" is basically fear of losing one's autonomy.

Some other emotions we know by various popular names are also expressions of these primary fears. If you track them down to their most basic levels, the basic fears show through.

Jealousy for example, is an expression of the fear of separation, or devaluation: "She'll value him more than she values me." At the extreme, it can express the fear of ego-death: "I'll be a worthless person."

Envy works the same way.

Shame and guilt express the fear, or the actual condition, of separation and even ego-death. The same is true for embarrassment and humiliation.

Fear is often the base emotion on which anger floats. Oppressed peoples rage against their oppressors because they fear, or actually experience, loss of autonomy and even ego-death. The destruction of a culture or a religion by an invading occupier may be experienced as a kind of collective ego-death.

Those who make us fearful will also make us angry.

Religious bigotry and intolerance may express the fear of ego-death on a cosmic level, and can even extend to existential anxiety. "If my god isn't the right god, or the best god, then I'll be stuck without a god. Without god on my side, I'll be at the mercy of the impersonal forces of the environment. My ticket could be cancelled at any moment, without a reason."

Some of our fears, of course, have basic survival value. Others, however, are learned reflexes that can be weakened or re-learned.

That strange idea of "fearing our fears" can become less strange when we realise that many of our avoidance reactions:

Turning down an invitation to a party if we tend to be uncomfortable in groups.

Putting off the doctor's appointment or not asking for the raise are instant reflexes that are reactions to the memories of fear. They happen so quickly that we don't actually experience the full effect of the fear. We experience a "micro-fear," a reaction that's a kind of shorthand code for the real fear. This reflex reaction has the same effect of causing us to evade and avoid as the real fear. This is why it's fairly accurate to say that many of our so-called fear reactions are actually the fears of fears.

When we let go of our notion of fear as the welling up of evil forces within us, the Freudian motif, and begin to see fear and its companion emotions as basically information, we can think about them consciously. And the more clearly and calmly we can articulate the origins of the fear, the less our fears frighten us and control us.

The enemy is fear. We think it is hate but its fear. ~ Gandhi

A few years ago I wrote a Blog called "Who's in the driver's seat." It came about because my beautiful, extremely talented ex-student who I'd trained as a dancer and was now Peak Performance Coaching was paralysed by fear. She'd auditioned for the 1st Season of the television series "So You Think You Can Dance" and didn't make it through to the Top 100.

And the reason she didn't make it to the Top 100 had nothing to do with lack of talent. The producers admitted that they had made the mistake of holding auditions in every other major city first so by the time they made it to Sydney they only had 20 spaces left. Nowhere near enough for one of the dance capitals of Australia.

When I asked my client if she was planning to audition for the 2nd Season she was hesitant. So I asked her what would stop her from auditioning again, and it turned out she was terrified that she wouldn't get through for a second time and that she'd have to face all of her peers that she'd studied full time with.

So I asked her what was more important? What her peers thought of her or going for something that she knew in her heart she really wanted to do? After a few coaching sessions, thankfully she decided to audition again and this time she sailed through to the top 100. Riding on that success she also got into a musical, so she decided to take that instead.

Fast forward a year or so and the same person found herself in a tricky situation. She'd landed a role in a musical that was going to be touring Asia, however she was also getting call back after call back for another musical that would be touring Australia. A call back means that the casting director is interested in seeing you do more. For example reading scripts, singing, picking up choreography etc.

Her agent tried to buy her time, but eventually she knew she had to make a decision. Did she accept the role she knew she already had, or did she continue to audition for the other one?

When she called me to ask me what to do I asked her a question. I said "which musical do you really want to be in?" And she told me it was the one she kept getting callbacks for. But I could hear the fear in her voice. She was feeling incredibly stressed and knew she had to make a decision. Should she accept the role that she knew she had or continue to audition for the musical she really wanted to be in? So I asked her "What's the worst case scenario?" And she said "Well that I say no to the musical that I know I've got and I don't get into the one that I really want."

I asked her, "what would happen then?" And she said "well I'd be really devastated." To which I replied "well, will you still have a roof over your head or will you be living on the street?" I knew at the time she was living with her mother so the later would not be the case. What I wanted her to recognise was that making her decision based on fear and scarcity wouldn't serve her in the future. So I asked her, "What would it take for you to back yourself? Are you willing to jump off the cliff so to speak and trust that you'll land on your feet? And what message will that send to the casting directors when they find out that you've turned down another musical because you're so committed to being in their musical?"

After a few deep breaths she decided to take fear out of her driver's seat and put both of her hands firmly on the wheel. So she graciously declined the musical she had successfully auditioned for and waited to hear if she'd been chosen for the other musical. As you can imagine that week was a tad nerve racking waiting, but I had faith that her decision to back herself would pay off. And it did! She landed a role in the musical of her choice.

And her self esteem, self worth and self confidence to make decisions that served her grew exponentially.

As that musical was coming to an end, she told me that she was sick of being in the chorus and playing the "swing" (the person who has to learn all the lead's parts) and that she deserved to have a lead role. That's when I knew that she was ready to claim what was rightfully hers. And she did. Not long after our conversation she landed one of the Lead Roles in *A Chorus Line* and toured all around Australia and Asia for over a year. Not only did she land a lead role, in every Theatre Critics Review she was singled out for her brilliant portrayal of her character.

I remember sitting in the audience with tears streaming down my face, arms covered in goosebumps as I watched her singing her solos and wowing the audience! She had finally realised that she was worth it. That she deserved to be successful!

The reason I've named this chapter "Who's in the Driver's Seat?" is because often people don't take control of their own lives. If you ask them why, they'll give you a myriad of reasons/excuses, but ultimately they all come down to one thing; FEAR. Fear of failing, fear of stuffing up in front of their peers, work mates, fear of looking silly, fear of being judged by others, fear of not being good enough, fear of change, and even fear of succeeding.

WHEN CAN FEAR SERVE US?

In some instances fear can actually serve us.

There are several cases where people have managed to lift incredibly heavy objects off people to save their lives. And then been dubbed "super human".

In the UK in June 2009 two mothers saved a schoolboy's life by lifting a 1.1 ton car off his body.

Donna McNamee and Abigail Sicolo sprang into action when the eight-year-old boy was run over outside their homes. Bailey Fowler was screaming in agony after he was trapped beneath the engine of the Renault Clio.

On hearing his screams, neighbours Miss McNamee, 24, and Miss Sicolo, 29, ran out and grabbed the car's bumper. They were then joined by Anthony McNamee, 47, Donna's father, who helped the two lift the car so the boy could be pulled free. Afterwards both women were surprised at managing to summon up the strength to lift the car. And their's is not a one off occurrence, there are many more cases of similar incidents.

Basically, what we have is a respectably large body of anecdotal evidence that suggests that in times of crisis, danger, or fear, some people have the ability to temporarily exercise superhuman strength.

The typical explanation given centres on adrenalin. Adrenalin, also called epinephrine, figures prominently in what's popularly called the "fight or flight" response.

Sudden stress, such as an impending fight or other dangerous situation, triggers the sympathetic nervous system to induce the fight or flight response, sometimes called hyper arousal or the acute stress response. It's a way that your body readies itself to deal with physical harm, very much like calling "Battle stations!" on a warship. The adrenal gland releases adrenalin into your bloodstream, and as it spreads throughout your body, it does different things to different types of tissue. Your airways relax to maximise breathing capacity, and metabolism increases. Your muscles go into glycolysis, which produces energy-rich molecules fuelling them for extraordinary action. While blood flow to the muscles is increased, blood flow to vulnerable extremities is decreased. Dopamine is produced in the brain as a natural pain killer. Peripheral vision turns into tunnel vision to minimise distractions. Reflexes and reaction times improve.

The brain structure which appears to be at the very

centre of most of the brain events associated with fear is the "amygdala" (Greek for "almond", its shape). It's our "fight or flight" response. And unfortunately when we're in that state the receptors in our brain freeze and we aren't able to function in a calm thoughtful manner.

> *We have nothing to fear but fear itself.*
> *-- Franklin Roosevelt*

Despite fear's amazing ability to energise individuals to superhuman feats, it can be incredibly limiting in blocking individuals from realising their dreams.

Have you heard the acronym for fear? F.E.A.R. = False Expectations Appearing Real.

Fear has stopped more people from living out their grandest life than any other limiting feeling.

As you are awakening, you are beginning to see fear for what it truly is. The only power fear ever has is the power that you give it. It is only through love that you can transform the paradigm.

THE VIBRATIONAL FREQUENCY OF FEAR

The definition of Vibrational Frequency is "The rate at which atoms and sub-particles of a being or object vibrate.

We're all made up of atoms, so every word we speak

and every thought we think sends out a vibration that attracts to it an experience of like vibration. If we send out fear, we attract fear. If we send out love, we attract love.

Each person has a unique vibration, which is the product of all of the influences he/she has ever encountered. The influences upon which we focus our attention or thoughts are those which determine or define our vibration.

Whatever we fear we usually create. For example: If you fear being alone, that's what you'll create. If you fear losing your job, you may well lose your job. If you fear failing, chances are you'll fail.

I had the pleasure of meeting a fellow Aussie, Paul Gelder, recently in LA. In February 2009 Paul was taking part in an Australian Navy counter-terrorism exercise in Sydney Harbour. Over dinner he shared with us his amazing story of being attacked by a Bull Shark. His courage to move forward with his life after having lost his arm and leg is beyond inspirational.

When Paul shared what happened that day he told us that the navy trains all of their divers to swim with their arms crossed at their chest. But on this particular day he thought to himself "I wonder what would happen if I put my hands by my side?" "I wonder if a shark would attack me." And of course it did. Which really reiterated for me how incredibly powerful our thoughts are.

Fear, unless its a life or death situation doesn't serve us. Fear sends out a vibrational frequency that attracts whatever we're fearing. Love on the other hand is the opposite of fear.

What I've learnt to do is not fear anything? And what shows up in my life is amazing. If I feel fear kicking in I acknowledge it, embrace it, take some deep breaths and recognise it as an opportunity to let it go and change my focus to trust, faith and love. In other words make fear my friend.

THE DIFFERENCE BETWEEN FEAR AND ANXIETY

Fear and anxiety both produce similar responses to certain dangers. But, many experts believe that there are important differences between the two.

Muscle tension, increased heart rate, and shortness of breath are a few of the physiological symptoms associated with a response to danger. These bodily changes occur due to an inborn flight or flight stress response that is believed to be necessary for our survival. Without this stress response, our mind wouldn't receive the alerting danger signal, and our bodies would be unable to prepare to flee or stay and battle when faced with danger.

Anxiety

According to authors Kaplan and Sadock, anxiety is, "a diffuse, unpleasant, vague sense of apprehension." It is often a response to an imprecise or unknown threat. For example, imagine you're walking down a dark street. You may feel a little uneasy and perhaps you have a few butterflies in your stomach. These sensations are caused by anxiety that is related to the *possibility* that a stranger may jump out from behind a bush, or approach you in some other way, and harm you. This anxiety is not the result of a known or specific threat. Rather it comes from your mind's vision of the possible dangers that may result in the situation.

Fear

Fear is an emotional response to a known or definite threat. Using the scenario above, let's say you're walking down a dark street and someone points a gun at you and says, "This is a stick up." This would likely elicit a response of fear. The danger is real, definite and immediate. There is a clear and present object of fear.

Although the focus of the response is different (real vs. imagined danger), fear and anxiety are interrelated. Fear causes anxiety, and anxiety can cause fear. But, the subtle distinctions between the two will give you a better understanding of your symptoms.

FEELING NERVOUS IS A GREAT SIGN

Nerves on the other hand are a sign that what you're about to do means a lot to you. If you speak to the most seasoned of performers they'll tell you that even after having performed in front of huge audiences for years they still feel nervous before they go on stage to perform. And believe me, that's a great thing!

Years ago I was standing in the wings of a theatre about to perform in a teacher's piece for the dance school I was teaching at. It was a medley of songs from the musical *A Chorus Line*. So here I was standing in the wings about to perform feeling unusually calm. I wasn't sure why, as every other time in my life I had been about to perform I had always experienced butterflies. But once I heard my music the butterflies would quickly disappear or transform into performance energy. So where were the butterflies now? As I entered on my cue I felt strange. Almost lethargic. I got through the number but I've got to say it was the most mediocre performance I'd ever given.

That experience was profound for me. It taught me so much that I was able to pass on to all of my students. The main thing was that nerves are our friend. They tell us that what we're about to do matters; that its important to us. All we need do is embrace them and transform them into performance energy. So I spent some time focusing on how I could teach my students to do precisely that.

That's when I came up with a process that we fondly called our Performance Bubble. No matter who we are, when we get nervous we forget to breath deeply. Instead taking short shallow breaths. Our shoulders lift and all of our energy is in the top half of our bodies. Especially around our head. And often our critical voice is having a field day, berating us, telling us we're going to stuff up etc. Can you relate?

So after testing the process with my students I decided to share it at a Tony Robbins Mastery University event in Aspen years ago when someone said they were terrified of falling and breaking a leg when they went skiing. I walked the whole audience through the steps and received amazing feedback. There were lots of trainers in the room and I'm guessing a lot of them added the process to their repertoire because its really created a ripple effect and I often hear trainers and coaches scattered all around the world using my process.

So I've outlined the steps below and you can use it in any context. Whether you're about to do a presentation at work, if you're going for a job interview, about to get married, going on a first date, really anytime you find yourself feeling nervous.

THE FIVE STEP PROCESS TO TRANSFORM YOUR NERVES

1. Choose a Performance Colour/s to suit the mood of what you're about to do.

2. Imagine the air around you is that colour. And breathe in that colour and see, feel and hear that colour making its way through your body all the way down to the soles of your feet.

3. Then see roots growing out of your feet going right down to the centre of the earth.

4. Put a a bubble of light around yourself in your Performance Colour/s

5. Check and see if you're still feeling nervous and if so take out your butterfly net and catch your butterflies. And put them in a V for victory formation, starting several inches below your navel and going right up to your waist.

Then go forth and do whatever it is you need to do, knowing that you've transformed your nervous energy into performance energy!

And please let me know how you go. Shoot me an email: kathryn@theconfidencecoach.net

I love receiving feedback and it also allows me to keep fine tuning the process.

So enough said about Fear, Anxiety and Nerves.

Where are you at in your life right now? Is fear in your Driver's Seat?"

BECOME YOUR #1 FAN

In your journal answer the following questions:

1. If you knew you couldn't fail, what would you do?
2. What one thing has been holding you back from doing what you wrote for the previous question?
3. What other dreams, hopes and desires have you given up on? And why?
4. What would it take for you to make whatever you answered in question 3 a priority and a reality?
5. What would you gain from achieving whatever you wrote in Question 3?
6. What are you waiting for? Often in life we tell ourself things like "oh the times not right. When _____ happens I'll _____. But if the truth be told, chances are the time will never be right. All we have however is right now, so why not start making your dreams, hopes and desires a reality?
7. What one thing can you do today before you go to sleep to start the process?

ACCOUNTABILITY

Accountability is a wonderful tool and a resource that doesn't cost a thing. If we keep our dreams, hopes and desires to ourselves then the only person who knows we're procrastinating or not taking the necessary actions to achieve them is ourselves.

However if we share those dreams, hopes and desires with other people it keeps us accountable. And on those days when it would be easier to sleep in, or worst still give up, just knowing someone else will know can be the perfect anecdote to keep moving us forward towards our goal.

So who can you trust to keep you accountable? Someone who will check in with you to see how you're progressing. And lovingly give you a kick in the butt if needs be?

MAKE FAILURE YOUR FRIEND

Fear of failing is often the reason why people don't achieve their goals. But the crazy thing is there are so many GIFTS in failing. As long as we're open to them. In fact it's the fastest way to achieve our goals. Fail fast, then review and correct, adjust your sails and take massive action. The people that achieve things in life know that failing is actually their friend. Yes you read correctly.

Years ago when I ran my School of Performing Arts I used to say to all my new students "Make lots of mistakes." And they'd look at me as if to say "Who is this crazy woman?" However when I explained that making mistakes was the fastest way to learn, they soon caught on and launched themselves full tilt into learning.

Unfortunately years of conditioning have taught us that failure is a bad thing. But its only bad if you don't learn from your mistakes and either keep making the same mistake over and over or give up.

Many years ago when I studied with Robert Kiyosaki he told us a story that really sums up what I'm talking about.

Imagine if you will, walking down a street on your way home and before you know it falling down a big pot hole that you weren't expecting. You hurt yourself, get up, dust yourself down and continue walking down the street until you arrive home battered and bruised. Tomorrow you walk home down that same street and ooops; before you know it you've fallen in that same pot hole again. Damn it!

At that moment you have two choices; keep repeating the pattern? Or learn from your mistake and either dodge the pot hole or perhaps choose to walk home down an entirely different street.

FAIL FAST AND FAIL FORWARD

Did you know that when a pilot flies a plane they're constantly reviewing and correcting? Most people think that the pilot hits the automatic pilot button, takes off and arrives at their destination. Not so. They're constantly reviewing and correcting.

Remember what I shared earlier about the team from Apollo 11 being "off course" for 93% of the time? However by constantly reviewing and correcting they reached their destination.

Unfortunately most of us give up if we're even 7% off track.

ITS TIME TO TAKE FEAR OUT OF THE DRIVER'S SEAT

BECOME YOUR #1 FAN

Take a moment now and imagine how amazing your life will be when you take fear out of your driver's seat and replace it with heartfelt determination, joy, perseverance and courage?

What is it your heart really desires? Be bold, be brave. Write it in your journal now and take baby steps every day until you've achieved it.

There's plenty of people throughout history that you can use as motivation. If it weren't for Thomas Edison, we may not have the luxury of light bulbs. When asked what motivated him to keep going after having failed so many times, he replied" "I have not failed 10,000 times. I have not failed once. I have succeeded in proving that those 10,000 ways will not work. When I have eliminated the ways that will not work, I will find the way that will work."

One of my favourite poems is by Goethe:

Until one is committed
There is hesitancy, the chance to draw back
Always ineffectiveness.
Concerning all acts of initiative (and Creation)
There is one elementary truth
The ignorance which kills countless ideas and splendid plans:
That the moment that one definitely commits ones self
Then Providence moves too.
All sorts of things occur to help one
That would never otherwise have occurred.
A whole stream of events issues from the decision
Raising in one's favour all manner
of unforeseen incidents and meetings
And material substance
Which no one could have dreamt
would have come your way.
Whatever you can do or dream you can, begin it.
Boldness has genius, power and magic in it.

CHAPTER NINE

Take Control of Your Life

YOU ARE 'ENOUGH'

As I discussed in earlier chapters, when we start to feel like we're flawed in some way we take on board all sorts of behaviors, to make sure we aren't rejected or laughed at by our family, friends and peers. The results are that acceptance by others becomes more important than self acceptance and can show up in numerous ways. Sometimes we become 'people pleasers' or good little girls or boys. And if we continue to ignore those feelings of not feeling we are 'enough' we start to compensate big time.

It's a bit like creating a huge hole in our self esteem and self worth and no matter what we try to fill it with, it just keeps seeping away.

I know someone who admits that she lacks self worth, but instead of working on learning to love herself she persists in trying to fill up that big hole with 'stuff.' She has more make up, more clothes, more jewelry, more shoes than she could ever wear in a lifetime. And yet she continues to buy more to make her self feel better. And the truth is she probably does get a quick fix in the moment she buys them. But all those things are never going to be 'enough' to fill up that hole and for her to feel like she is 'enough.'

The same person overeats, again trying to fill that big hole inside of herself. And then she battles with her weight. Which in turn robs her of the self esteem she does have and perpetuates the pattern of self destruction.

You may or may not be able to relate to this? Either way, please know that you are enough, and you knew that when you came into this world. You just forgot! It's time to remember.

LEARN TO SAY NO

As I mentioned in the previous paragraph, often times our lack of self esteem and self worth will cause us to become a 'people pleaser' putting others needs ahead of our own.

Most of us at some stage in our lives have said yes to someone when in actual fact we would have preferred to say no. Can you think of a time when this has happened to you? If so, try to recall why you didn't feel you could say no. Was it fear based? In other words, were you scared that the other person might not like your decision, or accept you? Or perhaps you were scared you would offend them?

Whatever the reason, when we say "yes," when we really mean "no," we are selling ourselves short, and for that matter the other person. Worst of all it has a negative impact on our Self Esteem, because we aren't honoring our own needs.

BECOME YOUR #1 FAN

Write down a situation that you found yourself saying "yes" instead of "no" to recently, and then practice by writing down a different response that honours your feelings while acknowledging the other person.

Scenario: _____

The question/invitation: _____

How you responded: _____

A more empowering response: _____

_____

So next time you have the opportunity, you might like to strengthen your emotional muscle, and say, "NO."

You can still be gracious by pre-empting your no with something like "thanks so much for the invitation however ...." or "I'd love to however......" That way the other person feels acknowledged while you've been true to your own feelings/wishes/desires. As you continue to do so your self esteem and confidence will soar!

DITCH THE HABITS THAT DON'T SERVE YOU

They say the definition of insanity is to continue doing the same thing over and over but expect a different outcome. Lots of people set New Year's Resolutions to lose weight, quit smoking, save money etc, but they aren't willing to ditch the habits that don't serve them in order to achieve their desired outcome.

Habits are just behaviours or thoughts that we feel comfortable doing because we've done them for so long. It requires no work on our behalf. But some of our habits really don't serve us. So how do we recognise which ones aren't serving us, ditch them and create new more empowering habits?

"We become what we repeatedly do."
~Sean Covey
The 7 Habits of Highly Effective Teens

The first step in ditching disempowering habits/be-haviours is to acknowledge them. Sometimes we're so busy doing our lives on automatic pilot, that we don't even realise that we're doing a behaviour that doesn't serve us. Similar to the analogy I used before about the mouse on the wheel, continuing to run around and around, but not really getting anywhere? Does that ring true for you? I know I've found myself doing exactly that, and yet expecting to get a different result! How crazy is that???

So in order to get a different result, we need to do a different behaviour/action. And yes the new behaviour or action may feel a bit (or maybe even a lot) uncomfortable at first! But over time it will become more comfortable.

Take a moment right now and cross your arms, and then look down and notice which arm is on top? Then try crossing your arms again, but this time put the other arm on top. Unless you're ambidextrous its bound to feel a bit uncomfortable!

If I asked you to brush your teeth with your less dom-inant hand you'd probably get toothpaste all over the place and not know exactly where one tooth starts and the next one begins. However if you stuck with it and used your less dominant hand for thrity days in a row, chances are it would start to feel more familiar.

It's the same when we want to change a habit. The other key to changing a habit that doesn't serve us is that we need to replace it with a more empowering one that still fills the initial need. So for example if you decide to give up smoking, you may find sucking on a lollipop fills the need to have something in your mouth. That said, you wouldn't want to be eating lollipops all day.

Often people will give up one addictive behaviour, only to replace it with another one e.g., give up smoking, but eat excessively, or drink alcohol excessively.

Sometimes we do behaviours to "mask" or cover up a deep-seeded fear or anxiety. So take a moment and think about a behaviour that you know doesn't serve you. It could be something as simple as the critical voice inside your head, or as complex as an addictive behaviour.

Just like in Chapter Six where we talked about replacing your negative self talk with a goofy, sexy or positive voice, we are far more likely to follow through with a new behaviour if it serves our deepest needs.

As my fiftieth birthday was fast approaching, I found that slowly but surely I was horrified to find I had put on 8 kilos or 17.6 pounds With my birthday a couple of months away I decided to use that as a motivator to get my eating "back on track". Sometimes having an impending event can be a great motivator to change a habit. It certainly was for me, as I was determined not to turn 50 feeling overweight and out of shape. So I joined the gym and starting watching what I ate. I joined Weight Watchers so that I was accountable.

How often do we decide we're going to do something different, and then just let life get in the way? I knew what would work for me, was if I had to front up to a meeting each week and get on the scales. I also decided to give myself treats, so that I didn't feel deprived. So each day my treat would be to have a skim milk cappuccino and instead of eating biscuits and chocolate in the evenings, I replaced it with fruit and liquorice. So I replaced the un-wanted behaviours with ones that served me but didn't leave me feeling like I had deprived myself.

RECOGNISE THE SECONDARY GAIN

All the behaviours we do are based on fulfilling a need. And often its the Secondary Gain that we get from doing something that keeps us stuck in old patterns.

For example one of my clients had been battling with her weight, and couldn't work out why she couldn't lose the excess pounds. It wasn't until we pin pointed her 'Secondary Gain' that she was able to finally lose her unwanted weight. Earlier in her life she'd experienced a very traumatic event. She was sexually abused and was terrified that it would happen again. So to dull down her beauty and make herself less attractive she stacked on lots of weight. Which in turn made her feel safer. When she understood that she didn't need to do that any more the weight (which is often a protective coating) fell off.

Take a moment now and think about something you're not having success achieving. By not achieving it, what's the pay off or secondary gain? There's always something. Sometimes its obvious and other times you might have to do some detective work on yourself to reveal what's really going on.

Once you can identify what the pay off or secondary gain is you can choose to get that need met in a more empowering way, which in turn will free you up to focus on achieving your goal or outcome.

Well known Motivational Facilitator, Success Coach and Author, Anthony Robbins has created a list of emotional needs that are commonly known as "The Six Human Needs". He is not referring to the basic survival needs for example, water, food, shelter etc. The needs that he refers to are the "emotional needs" we require as individuals. And some of them are contradictory

His theory is that all human behaviour is driven by the instinct to fulfil one or more of the six fundamental human needs and are the driving force behind every human being and their motivation levels.

THE SIX HUMAN NEEDS

Certainty or Comfort

The need for the feeling that everything is settled, secure, and that there are no nasty surprises around the corner. The ability to avoid pain and gain pleasure.

Uncertainty or Variety

The precise opposite, and potentially in conflict with the need for Certainty. The need to feel that life is interesting, diverse, exciting and challenging. If relationships become totally predictable and certain, sometimes one member will pick a fight, or be unfaithful merely to create some excitement and spontaneity which in turn feeds their need for uncertainty.

Love and Connection

The need to feel love from and for, and connection with others. The need to bond, experience intimacy, to feel oneness.

Significance

The need to feel that you have meaning to others, you are unique, special, important. (NB: potential conflict with the need for Love and Connection)

Everyone, without exception, finds a way to get these first four needs fulfilled, even if it is in a very low quality and sometimes negative way. Just think about when a child doesn't receive the positive attention they need from a parent. They will do whatever it takes to get their needs met. They may act out, throw a tantrum, be blatantly disobedient etc. but ultimately they get their parents attention and fulfil that need.

As adults, we do the same thing. Unhappiness, emotional distress and dysfunctional behaviour can arise from an individual's inability to find a consistent way to meet his/her Six Human Needs in a positive way.

For instance, the compelling, overwhelming need for Love and Connection explains why someone will stay in an abusive relationship. As terrible as the abuse is, it is a form of connection. Without appropriate help the individual chooses to stay, over the uncertainty of leaving, with the fear of living without any kind of connection.

The fifth and sixth needs are not met by everyone, yet their consistent attainment is the key to a life of fulfilment. Survival is possible, indeed common, without fulfilling these two needs. The life you want and deserve, however, is not.

Growth

The need for the feeling that we are growing, intellectually, spiritually, physically.

Contribution

The need to feel that we are giving of ourselves for the benefit of other living things. In other words that we are contributing to life itself.

Everyone has their own unique requirements for the fulfilment of each of the six human needs. The degree to which those requirements are being met in a positive, high quality and sustainable way defines the overall quality of their life.

Some people get their needs met in a destructive or negative way. For example they may use alcohol, cigarettes or drugs to feel "relaxed" for the moment. While others may choose to meet that need by meditating, going shopping, having sex, reading a book. The number of ways to fulfil this need is as unlimited as the number of people who use them.

But remember, you choose the way in which to have your needs met, it does not choose you!

BECOME YOUR #1 FAN

Take a moment now to think about how you get your Six Human Needs met? Create a quiet space where you won't be interrupted and in your journal, make headings for the "Six Human Needs".

Underneath each heading, take a look at the various areas of your life for example: primary relationship, family, friends, hobbies and career. Jot down all the ways that you create certainty, uncertainty, significance, connection/love, contribution and growth in your life.

Then, ask yourself the question. Am I getting my needs met in a positive or negative way?

Go back and colour code each answer. Choose a colour for meeting your needs in a positive way, and then a different colour for meeting them in a negative way. Or alternatively, you might like to put a tick next to the positives and a cross next to the negatives.

Take a moment to observe how much of your life is being directed by you in a positive, life affirming way, and how much is being met in a negative/destructive way?

If you find you are getting your needs met in a destructive way, ask yourself, what could I do differently to have these needs met in a positive way? What would I need to believe/appreciate or do, in order to feel more fulfilled in this category now? You might like to brainstorm some ideas and jot them down. Sometimes it can be useful to ask someone that you know and trust, how they perceive your behaviours/ actions.

When you're building a new attitude and way of being it's crucial to check in and ensure that the new attitude or behaviour serves your needs in positive ways.

TIME FOR A TUNE UP?

Most of us service our cars on a regular basis because we know that they'll work more effectively and last longer if we look after them. But how often do we put our Mind Set, Beliefs and Behaviours in for a service?

Some of you might be old enough to remember a great song from the 80's by Patti LaBelle called "New Attitude." For those of you that aren't familiar with the song the lyrics go like this:

Running, hot, running cold, I was running
into overload, it was extreme.

It took me so high, so low, so low there was nowhere to go, like a bad dream.

Somehow the wires got crossed, the tables were turned, I never knew I had such a lesson to learn.

I'm feeling good from my head to my shoes, know where I'm going and I know what to do, I tidied up my point of view I'VE GOT A NEW ATTITUDE!

I'm in control, my worries are few, 'cause I got love like I never knew, ooh, ooh, ooh, ooh, I'VE GOT A NEW ATTITUDE!

I'm wearing a new dress, new hat, brand new ideas as a matter of fact, I've changed for good.

It must have been the cool night, new moon, slight change. More than to figure, oh but I feel like I should say yes.

I gotta a new, new attitude. Ooh, ooh, ooh, ooh, ooh. Everything about me has changed.

Baby I ain't the same, I gotta new attitude.
I gotta a brand new, brand new, ooh, ooh,
ooh, ooh, I'VE GOT A NEW ATTITUDE!

Have you ever heard the saying "it all comes down to attitude?" Most of us don't realise that before we get out of bed each day, we're setting up what type of day we are going to have. Now I know that sounds crazy, and some of you are probably saying "but I can't control what other people do" and you're absolutely right. We can't control everything that happens in our day, even though we might like to. Just the same as we can't change what's happened in the past, **but we can control how we respond versus react to any given situation and we're in charge of the meaning we give it.**

"Change the way you look at things and the things you look at change." ~ Wayne Dyer

I shared in the introduction how I allowed someone to break my heart so badly which left me feeling so rejected that I decided I was unworthy of love and didn't want to live. And that was by far the scariest thing that I've ever had to deal with. But in the moment that I chose to live, I decided to use the experience to transform my life. I decided that if my beautiful students and their parents loved me, then perhaps it was time for me to learn to love me, from the inside out.

So what appeared to be my biggest nightmare, became my biggest opportunity and in the end my biggest gift!

Now I don't know what you're dealing with in your life right now, but what I do know is that the meaning we give to things determines the emotions and behaviours that we then experience. In NLP we call them "Frames".

FRAMES

There's a term in NLP called Frames. Just like the frames we put around a picture or portrait to compliment it, we're constantly putting frames around things that happen in our lives to give them meaning.

WE DECIDE WHAT IS REAL

Here's a diagram below that explains what I mean.

WHAT WE FOCUS ON	=	OUR REALITY
THE MEANING WE GIVE SOMETHING	=	DETERMINES THE EMOTIONS WE FEEL
THE EMOTIONS WE FEEL	=	DETERMINES THE BEHAVIOURS WE DO
THE BEHAVIOURS WE DO	=	PRODUCES A RESULT

So if we want to create a different result we have to go back and change the meaning we give something.

As I write this, there are thousands, if not millions, of people that have decided that we are in a Global Recession. The meaning that they have given to the economic downturn is a very different meaning to the one that I have given it.

I believe that as a planet we were spinning out of control. Environmentally, economically and emotionally. We had lost sight of the most important aspect of life. Material possessions, greed and power were ruling our world as we knew it. So we really needed to have a crisis of some sort to make us sit up, listen, and decide to do things differently. Which in turn will bring us back into alignment and hopefully secure the future of our beautiful planet.

So two entirely different points of view/meaning for what is happening at the moment.

I know that if we focus on the belief that "we are in a recession" then we'll breathe life into it, and that is what we'll experience. On the other hand, if we refuse to call it a recession and instead call it a "Rebalancing of our highest values" then we can see it for the gift it is. An opportunity to learn, grow and embrace change (even though it may be extremely uncomfortable).

It reminds me of two stories that emphasise the meaning we give to things. One is a one line poem and it goes like this:

"Two men looked through prison bars: one saw mud, the other stars"

Both men were in prison. One focused on how bad it was and the other focused on how he was going to change his life when he was released from prison.

Nelson Mandella is an example of exactly that. He is a true visionary that stood up for equal rights in South Africa way before the majority of the white population were ready to hear it. Undeterred, he was sentenced to life imprisonment because he stood up for what he believed.

He spent 27 years in jail and when they asked him how he stayed sane all that time, he said that he knew that if he didn't do something every day to use his brain and his body he would literally go insane. So he spent his time working out physically, reading and focusing on what he would do when he got out. Four years after he was released from prison he became South Africa's first Black President.

He recently turned 95 and on July 18, 2008 at a concert to celebrate his 90th Birthday Mandella said:

"Where human beings are being oppressed, there is more work to be done. Our work is for freedom for all. It is time for new hands to lift the burdens. It is in your hands now. I thank you."

THE KEY TO BUILDING A NEW ATTITUDE, BELIEF OR BEHAVIOUR

- Acknowledge the old way of being and then find a way to let it go. You might like to write it down and then scribble all over it "I don't need you anymore" then go ahead and rip it up and throw it in the garbage, or you might prefer to scream it in your head or out loud.

- Use Winning Words like, Yet, up until now, in the past, to set yourself up for success

- Acknowledge that it will probably feel uncomfortable, but by persevering over time it will feel more comfortable

- Try to make it fun

- Create an "impending event" to give you momentum. For example your birthday, the date you plan to go on holiday or a family celebration. Remember the impetus for me to shed the weight I'd gained was me turning 50.

- Realise that there is no such thing as failure, only feedback!

- If you go off track, be gentle on yourself, review and correct until you're back on track

- Do it for at least 30 days

- Who we hang out with, is who we become! So make it easier by spending time with people that already do the new behaviour, attitude or way of being.

DIRECTIONALISE YOUR LANGUAGE

Often we can get caught up focusing on what we DON'T want versus what we do want. While life circumstances teach us what we don't want to experience again be it a relationship, a job, our health etc., it's far more important to focus on what we DO want.

This little experiment below will show you exactly what I mean:

- DON'T picture a pink elephant
- And DON'T look down and see that its wearing a pair of shiny silver tap shoes
- And DON'T notice that it has a pink and purple polka dotted ribbon tied in a bow on its tail
- And definitely DON'T look at its head and see that its wearing a big green hat with an orange daisy attached.

What happened? I bet you saw all of those things? How often do we hear a parent telling a child what they DON'T want them to do, for example; DON'T spill the milk, DON'T speak to me that way, DON'T forget etc.....

When a far more productive way of communicating would be to say what we DO want for example:

- I know you can carry that milk jug successfully to the table
- Please speak respectfully
- Remember to....................

Its a bit like drawing out our bow and arrow and pointing it at the bulls eye. So remember, focus on what you do want.

THE POWER OF YOUR WORDS

Similar to the previous paragraph about directionalising your language, there are some words that create an emotional sense of lack or deprivation. And lets face it, who wants to deprive themselves? Most human beings are wired to move away from pain and towards pleasure. So if you have a goal to lose weight, I recommend you replace the word "lose" weight with the word "release." I.e., I easily and effortlessly release 20 unwanted kilos of body weight that no longer serve me, by always giving myself the gift of nutritious delicious meals and snacks.

SETTING AND GETTING GOALS

Part of taking control of your life is about believing in yourself enough to set and achieve goals. The following S.M.A.R.T. Model Below is a great tool to help you not only set goals, but also achieve them.

S. SPECIFIC
M. MEASURABLE
A. ACHIEVABLE
R. RELEVANT
T. TIME FRAME

One of the keys to achieving your goals is to break them down into smaller achievable goals. That way it won't feel overwhelming. Each small goal then serves as a stepping stone towards your bigger goal which I refer to as your outcome. And in turn creates a sense of achievement. You've probably heard the phrase "Success breeds success." By breaking your goals down into bite sized achievable pieces you're creating a strong foundation for success, which will in turn will create the emotions that will catapult your forward to achieving your next goal and eventually your major outcome.

For example if your outcome is to release 20 kilos your smaller bite sized chunks/goals could be to lose 1 kilo per week.

ASK YOURSELF:

- What exactly do I want?
- Where, with whom and when, specifically do I want this outcome?
- Can I achieve this outcome by myself, or do I need the actions and behaviours of others first?
- How will I know when I have achieved my outcome? What will be my evidence procedure?
- How else can I achieve my outcome?

STEP ONE

Write your goal in the positive, keep it short, concise and specific. Write it as if you have already achieved it, starting with your name or I. Be sure to state what you do want versus what you don't want. It should be measurable and an appropriate size. It should also be self initiated and self maintaining i.e.,not reliant on someone other than yourself.

Can you create a detailed mental experience (sight, sound and feelings) of what it will be like once your outcome is achieved?

Enter your Outcome Description

_____

_____

_____

STEP TWO
Expected Completion Date

_____

STEP THREE – Step up to your Meta outcome? The Meta Outcome is the one that hovers above your goal and is usually the driving force to achieve your desired outcome. What does achieving your goal give you? In my instance shedding my excess weight allowed me to wear the type of clothes I enjoyed wearing and I also felt fitter, stronger and better about myself.

Ask yourself:

- For what purpose do I want this outcome?
- What will this outcome get for me?
- What does my outcome really mean to me?
- Ask yourself, once I've achieved my outcome, what will it have done for me?

_____

_____

_____

STEP FOUR – Is your outcome ecological? In other words, is achieving your outcome not only good for you, but is it good for the greater good? For those around you and the environment?

Ask yourself:

- Am I ADDING CHOICE rather than taking it away?
- Are there any contexts of my life when having this outcome would NOT work well for me?
- Where do I want this outcome to be present?
- Where don't I want this outcome to be present?
- How can I modify my outcome so that it works in all contexts?
- If I got my outcome straight away would I take it?

These considerations alert you to issues you will need to attend to as you are achieving your outcome.

STEP FIVE

What are your beliefs about the outcome?

- Is my outcome really what I want?
- Do I have any beliefs that might limit my success in achieving my outcome?
- What would be a more empowering way to think about my outcome?
- Do I believe I can achieve my outcome?
- What are more empowering beliefs I want to emphasise?
- Do I believe it will be easy to achieve my outcome?

Are all of your beliefs POSITIVE and SUPPORTIVE of your outcome? If NOT then either CHANGE YOUR BELIEFS, to support the direction of your outcome, or rewrite your outcome to be more believable.

Enter your beliefs about the outcome, for example:

- Is it achievable?
- Is it realistic?
- Is it the right size?

You should explore all your beliefs around your outcome, both positive and negative, especially including those beliefs which might limit you or not support you fully in achieving your outcome.

BELIEFS ABOUT THE OUTCOME – Negative and Positive

STEP SIX

What might prevent you?
Ask yourself:

- What are the benefits and secondary gain of the present state? How can I achieve my outcome and maintain my benefits?
- What prevents me from having my desired outcome NOW?
- What can I do to overcome any possible limitations?
- What are the most crucial elements of achieving my outcome? What might prevent these?

These considerations alert you to the issues you will need to attend to as you are achieving your outcome?

Enter any limitations or things that might stop you from achieving your outcome. Ask yourself, "What stops me or might prevent me from achieving my outcome? You should explore all the 'benefits' (secondary gains) of the present state, determining whether your outcome preserves all of the secondary benefits. Those benefits not preserved may prevent you from fully achieving your outcome.

1. _____
2. _____
3. _____
4. _____
5. _____
6. _____

STEP SEVEN

What Resources are needed?

Ask yourself:

- What resources do I need to achieve my outcome"
- Imagining that I have already achieved my outcome, what did need along the way?
- What resources have I used in similar situations?
- What resources have other people used in similar situations?

- What internal resources would be most useful?

Enter the resources necessary to achieve your outcome, for example: training, materials, skills, people etc… You should list all those resources you will need to obtain or gather in order to achieve your outcome.

_____

_____

_____

_____

_____

_____

STEP EIGHT

Step down to Short Term Goals
Ask yourself:

- What do I need to achieve my desired outcome?
- Is my first goal or first step easily and completely achievable?
- Are all my goals positive and expressed positively?
- Is each goal or step of an appropriate size? If not then do a separate outcome for those that are too large.

These considerations alert you to the issues you will need to attend to as you are achieving your outcome.

Enter short term goals that easily lead you to your outcome. Break your outcome into smaller, easily achievable steps, so that each short term goal is of an appropriate size, set within an appropriate time frame and so that you are easily guided from success to success in achieving your outcome.

STEP DOWN:
TO SHORT TERM GOALS   Expected Completion Date

_____

_____

_____

_____

Are all your goals easily achieved and of an appropriate size, guiding you swiftly in the direction of your outcome?

Have you created a detailed mental experience (sight, sounds and feelings) of what it will be like once each goal is achieved?

IF YOU HAVE ANSWERED NO TO ANY OF THESE QUESTIONS, THEN PLEASE ADJUST YOUR GOALS.

And remember to celebrate like crazy every time you achieve one or your short term goals, because that will juice you up to forge ahead and ultimately achieve the big one!

ASK YOURSELF:

What can I do right now to begin achieving my Outcome Today!

_____

_____

_____

_____

RECOGNISING SABOTAGE PATTERNS

Sometimes when we set goals or outcomes we'll allow ourselves a degree of success but when it comes to achieving that really big outcome or goal that we're really going for, we end up sabotaging it. Can you relate? I know I've done it and its a recurring pattern of behaviour that I see in a lot of my clients.

One young dancer I was coaching a few years ago had auditioned and gotten call backs for both the Royal Ballet and the English National Ballet. I met her about 2 weeks before she was due to fly to London for her call-backs. And at that stage she was riddled with self doubt and couldn't really believe she'd gotten a call back. So we set about releasing all of her negative beliefs and replacing them with empowering ones. After a couple of one-on-one sessions she was in a totally different frame of mind. We Re-Framed the purpose of the audition, and instead of focusing on the fact that she was auditioning and hoping that she was good enough to be accepted by her first choice, the Royal Ballet, we decided to flip it around. Instead she was going to audition the Royal Ballet School to see if in fact the school was a good fit for her. As I mentioned earlier, the meaning we give something has a huge impact on how we feel, and those feelings drive our behaviours which in turn produce a result. So off she went having written her script for exactly how she wanted the trip to go! And voila! She got accepted into both companies and decided to take up her place at the Royal Ballet.

As you can imagine, she was beside herself with joy. However, after the initial elation wore off and she returned to Sydney to continue taking classes until lshe took up her position in London, she'd started "comfort eating" and putting on weight. Thankfully we caught it early on, and I explained that when deep down we don't feel we deserve something, we'll often sabotage it. So it was a sign for us to do more work on building her self esteem and self worth. And thankfully she did and flew off to London and took up her position at the Royal Ballet School.

So while affirmations, and script writing and visualising your desired outcome are all wonderful tools, they won't produce the results you're after unless you really believe you deserve them.

As tiny babies, we knew we were worthy. We knew

our needs were important. So reconnecting with our Inner Child is an important step in taking control of our lives and achieving our goals.

LET GO OF THE "HOW"

The other thing I've learnt over the last 20 years or so is that often I don't need to know "how" I'm going to achieve something. In fact sometimes all I need to do is get clear on what I want to achieve and then get out of my own way.

I know when we decided that we would relocate to live in Hawaii, I really didn't know exactly "how" that would happen. And there were plenty of people telling me it was impossible to get a visa, that it was hard, that I'd never achieve it in the time frame I'd decided on etc.....

I just knew from previous experience that somehow it would all work out and we'd end up being able to relocate. And we did. I ended up getting a B1 Visa for five years (which my Immigration Lawyer here in the US says is unheard of) and my daughter got an F1 Visa to study full time. And then this year I went on to win the US Green Card Diversity Lottery.

Living our lives in a state of positive anticipation just like when we were tiny babies is a very powerful way to be.

ROAD BLOCKS ARE OFTEN DIVINE GUIDANCE

The other thing I've learnt is when obstacles or road blocks seem to be stopping me from doing/being or having something, it's usually because the universe/god/ buddha whatever you like to call is has a better plan. So instead of getting angry or frustrated that things aren't going according to my plan, I take a few deep breaths and literally surrender myself to the process.

As I mentioned in an earlier chapter, when I was 21 I flew to the UK to be with my english boyfriend I'd met in Australia. As it turned out, he flew out to the US for six months on exactly the same day that I flew in to be with him. So I toured the UK with my girlfriend that I'd travelled over with. And then when we arrived back in London I decided to take a dance class. And loved it. Long story short, I ended up auditioning to attend the school full time and achieved my dream of becoming a Professional Dancer. One that I might add I'd given up on ever happening. So that experience taught me to trust that life will lead me where I need to go. And sometimes it takes me getting out of my own way!

"We make plans and god laughs"
~ Old Yiddish Proverb

OPEN YOUR #1 FAN BANK ACCOUNT

Just like the analogy I used earlier about having an in-finite amount of balloons when we are born, that represent our self esteem, I'd like you to imagine that you have a bank account. Not a traditional bank account. More like an emotional bank account that represents your Self Esteem, Self Worth and Self Confidence.

Every time you put yourself down or do something that negates who you are, you're making a withdrawal from your bank account. On the flip side, every time you compliment yourself, re-program your negative self talk, try on a new behaviour or attitude or celebrate a win, you're putting a deposit into your bank account.

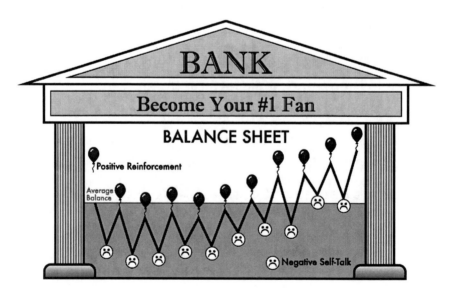

"You yourself, as much as anybody in the entire universe, deserve your love and affection" ~ Gautama Buddha

While some of you might feel like there isn't much in your bank account right now, or that it's in the red, the great news is, that you can change that right now, by simply acknowledging that you are ready and willing to change. The fact that you are reading this book, shows me that you are interested in feeling great about yourself.

Chances are, you've probably been tough on yourself up until now, so find ways every day to make a deposit. Or going back to my balloon analogy, blow up a balloon. If you do this every day for 30 days, imagine how many more balloons and bank deposits you will have? And how much better you'll feel about yourself?

Some of my clients have celebrated by literally blowing up a real balloon every time they treated themselves with more respect. And having the balloons up in your home or work environment is a wonderful reminder to celebrate who you are along with your wins.

30 DAYS TO INSTIL A NEW BEHAVIOUR

Research shows that by consistently doing a new behaviour for 30 days, we are far more likely to continue doing the new behaviour.

BECOME YOUR #1 FAN

Get out your calendar and choose one new behaviour that you are going to do or say right now. Write it down in your journal or on a piece of paper and put it up somewhere as a reminder. Each time you do it, make a tick on your calendar! After the 30 days, if the new behaviour is working for you, continue to do it, if not discard it and try another one!

RECEIVING AND GIVING COMPLIMENTS

In Australia (where I grew up) we aren't that great yet at receiving compliments graciously. I think it probably stems way back, and based on how our original colonies were formed. Aside from the original custodians of our land (the Aboriginals) everyone else came from somewhere else, primarily England. And most of the initial settlers were convicts who had been banished to a supposedly desolate land as punishment for petty crimes like stealing a loaf of bread to feed their family. I believe that as a nation, we've never rid ourselves of the guilt and shame of our history and that forms the core of our "We're not good enough mentality".

Australians seem to measure their success by constantly comparing themselves with other countries. We look to America for acknowledgement that we have great actors, singers, dancers etc.

So I believe we're way overdue in claiming back our self esteem as a nation!

Wherever we live, most of us find it really hard to accept a compliment. Someone goes to the trouble of giving us one, and instead of receiving it graciously, we say things like "What this old dress, oh my hair is actually dirty" or something else that blocks or negates the compliment.

It ends up being a lose/lose situation, because the person giving it, feels their compliment is unappreciated, and the person receiving it hasn't got the self esteem to graciously accept the compliment by simply saying "thank you."

So next time someone pays you a compliment get into the habit of looking the person in the eye and saying "Thank you".

There's a wonderful saying "Attitudes are contagious." So give the people you care about genuine compliments, and in the process coach them on how to accept them graciously.

I make it a priority to give at least one person a compliment each day. I remember telling a lady that worked at a checkout counter at our local supermarket that she had beautiful blue eyes, and she lit up like a Christmas Tree!

Just imagine how great we'll all feel when we start giving and receiving genuine compliments on a daily basis?

COMPLIMENTS BOXES

Making "Compliments Boxes" is a lovely activity to do with friends, work colleagues and/or family. We often find it easier to give someone else a compliment than to give one to ourselves. So doing this as a Group Activity is a great way to get started.

BECOME YOUR #1 FAN

You can use any type of small box. I like to go to craft shops and buy small heart or star shaped paper mache boxes. That way after you've done the Compliments Activity you can decorate your box however you like, to make it uniquely yours. You can paint it, decorate it with glitter, sparkles, collage cut outs etc. You'll also need some blank paper cut up into small rectangular pieces approximately 6 cm or 2.5 inches wide and 3 cm or 1.5 inches deep. Make sure you have enough for everyone in the group to write at least two compliments for each person including themselves.

Sit in a circle, with your boxes in front of you. Take the lid off your box and ask everyone in the circle to use their pieces of paper to write a compliment for everyone in the circle including themselves. It might be about a skill, personality trait, behaviour, physical appearance or something you admire about them. Make it anonymous as that makes it easier to receive and even more special just knowing that someone feels that way about you. And once you've written it, fold the paper in two so the compliment isn't showing write the person's name on the outside and place it in the person's box. Make sure that everyone does at least 2 for each person in the group before they open their own box and read their compliments.

Then make it a ritual to read all your compliments in the morning to set yourself up for a wonderful day. Alternatively when your ego has taken a beating and you're not feeling so great about yourself, opening your compliments box and reading the compliments can help to lift your mood and remind you of how special you really are!

CHAPTER TEN

Creating the Life of Your Dreams

If you skipped straight to this chapter I suggest you go back and read the rest of the book first. Without a doubt there are some incredibly valuable tools and resources in this chapter. However, they will all be useless unless you develop your awareness, your self esteem, self worth and self belief. For example you can affirm being prosperous, successful in your career or finding the man or women of your dreams until the cows come home. But unless you believe you deserve it, your efforts will be in vain.

I highly recommend you go back and read each chapter, doing each of the exercises as you go. That way you'll be evolved enough and ready to really get the gold that these last two chapters contain.

CLARITY IS THE KEY

In order to live the life of your dreams, you need to get clear on how you want your life to be. Unfortunately, most people spend more time planning their holidays than they do planning their lives. How revealing is that?

Often people set goals for themselves and wonder why they never achieve them. And often its because their goals/outcomes aren't aligned with their highest values..

GAIN CLARITY ON YOUR VALUES

Once we are clear on our values, what's important to us, we can make the majority of our decisions based on those values. Having clear values and making choices based on them, not only builds our Self Esteem and Self Confidence, it propels us forward to create the future we dream of.

Below is an exercise to explore some values and identify what's important to you. A list of common values have been provided for you below.

BECOME YOUR #1 FAN

Review the list and select the top ten values that are the most important to you.

Consider which values serve as guides for how you behave, or are important components of how you want to live your life. If you think of any other values that aren't on this list, you can still make them part of your list of top ten values.

You might like to highlight all of the ones that resonate with you and then narrow them down to your Top Ten.

Adventure

Advancement

Arts

Challenging problems

Cleanliness, orderliness

Commitment

Community

Competition

Contentment

Cooperation

Customer satisfaction

Achievement

Affection

Calm, quietude, peace

Change and Variety

Close relationships

Communication

Competence

Concern for others

Continuous improvement

Creativity

Democracy

Development	Discipline
Ecological awareness	Economic security
Equality	Efficiency
Ethical practice	Excellence
Excitement	Faith
Fame	Family
Feeling	Flair
Friendship	Honour
Hard work	Harmony
Honesty	Innovation
Integrity	Intellectual status
Involvement	Loyalty
Love and romance	Leadership
Maximum utilisation (time)	Meaningful work
Merit	Money
Nature	Openness
Optimal health	Order
Perfection	Personal growth
Preservation	Pleasure
Recognition	Religion
Responsibility	Resourcefulness
Respect for individuals	Results Driven
Responsiveness	Reputation
Self-giving	Self-reliance
Service (to others)	Security

Self respect	Serenity
Simplicity	Sophistication
Speed	Spiritual life
Strength	Stability
Status	Systemization
Success	Teamwork
Time freedom	Tolerance
Tradition	Truth
Trust	Wealth
Wisdom	Work
Working with others	Working alone

VALUES HIERARCHY

Once you have identified your 'top ten" values, it's time to put them into a hierarchy format for example, most important = 1 least important = 10 and list them below.

Often this takes some time to ponder, so what I suggest you do is write down each value on a separate post it note. Then put them up on a whiteboard or mirror in the order you think they might go, and each day spend a bit of time playing with the order. I know when I did this exercise my post it notes moved around considerably until they landed in a place that I felt was spot on.

And it's also a fun exercise to revisit at different stages of our lives. I know my values changed quite dramatically when I became a mother. Ultimately we choose to spend our time based on our highest values.

So if you have a goal that isn't aligned with your highest values its highly likely you won't achieve it. If the goal is important to you, then you may need to re-arrange your values? Once you feel you have your values in order write them down below:

My Top Ten Values

1. _____
2. _____
3. _____
4. _____
5. _____
6. _____
7. _____
8. _____
9. _____
10. _____

CREATING A VISION OF HOW YOU WANT YOUR FUTURE TO BE

Often we can get caught up doing our lives on "automatic pilot". Similar to a mouse on a wheel, running around and around but not getting anywhere.

In order to get a different outcome, we need to do something different. Having a clear vision of where we're heading, gives us a sense of purpose.

As mentioned previously in the Internal Locus of Control, when we are self directing and take responsibility for our actions, we automatically develop confidence in ourselves and our ability to create the life we want. So what do you want for yourself in the future?

There are several ways you can do this:

1. Write yourself a letter from the future.
2. Create a Vision Board
3. Make a Mind Movie.

You might like to try all of them or alternatively decide which one appeals to you?

BECOME YOUR #1 FAN

LETTER FROM THE FUTURE

Choose a date some months or even years ahead, a date that means something to you, an anniversary or a birthday. Then imagine your life has gone rather well. Things have turned out the way you wanted them to. Write a letter telling yourself about the developments in your life. Try to imagine how your life would feel if you were successful and fulfilled.

Another way of creating your vision is to visualise how you want it to be. If this appeals to you, then you might like to take a moment to stop and think about what you want. Some people find closing their eyes works, while others prefer to look up and off to the right. Whatever works for you, take a moment now to visualise how you want your future to be. The key is to be as specific as possible. Really stimulate all your senses:

~ What have you achieved?

~ What do you see, what do you hear inside your head and around you?

~ How do you feel? Include your sense of smell and taste.

Once you have a clear vision, write it all down in a journal, or notebook, or even on your computer and write it as if you were writing a script for a movie. And **be sure to write it in Past Tense** as if its already happened. Once you have it all down, read it every morning before you get out of bed, and in the evening before you go to sleep.

If you don't enjoy writing you might like to make a Vision Board/Poster? Or in my case do both.

MAKING YOUR VISION BOARD/POSTER

You'll need a large piece of cardboard, if you're very artistic you might like to draw your images, otherwise if you're like me, you might like to cut out key words and pictures from magazines and glue them onto your cardboard. Or alternatively use a combination of both. Have fun with it and feel free to use stickers to make your board as beautiful as possible. And be sure to include a picture of yourself in the middle of the board.

Once it's made, put your vision board/poster in a spot that you will see a lot. I have mine in my bedroom so that I can see it as I wake up and go to sleep. Which by the way is the most powerful time to access our unconscious mind, which ultimately rules the show. You might however prefer to have it in your bathroom, office or school locker? Just do whatever works best for you.

I made a Vision Board a couple of years ago when we lived in Sydney (and way before I had the slightest notion that we'd be relocating to Hawaii) A few weeks before we were due to fly out a dear friend pointed out to me that a lot of the images I'd chosen for my Vision Board looked as though they were taken in Hawaii. So in my experience, this stuff works! I'm sure you've heard the saying "be careful what you wish for?" Well thats especially true when making your Vision Board.

MAKE A MIND MOVIE

Mind Movies are an extremely powerful tool as you can choose images (either yours or the ones provided) that are aligned with your Vision for the Future and add affirmations and music so you end up with your own Vision for the Future Movie that stimulates all of your senses.

I love this wonderful tool and I've made several different ones for different areas of my life i.e: relationship, career, health, family. You can use their images, your images or a combination of both. And the same goes for the affirmations. And then you get to choose what music to have in the background. Its very cool.

Here's the link to the website where you can make your own. And to get you started immediately you might like to use their pre-made one's? They focus on the 6 key areas of life: Wealth, relationships, attracting the perfect woman, attracting the perfect man, spiritual fulfillment and health and fitness.

http://www.mindmovies.com/bonuses/signup-bonus.php?26192

Once you've downloaded and/or made your movie, be sure to watch it the moment you open your eyes in the morning and last thing at night.

Within a week of making my first Prosperity Mind Movie I received an unexpected cheque for several thousand dollars in the mail. And was blown away as one of the images I'd included in my Prosperity Movie was that money came to me from unexpected sources. I also noticed in one of my Mind Movies I had pictures of Hawaii, and voila! Guess where we live now? Heavenly Honolulu. So this stuff works (as long as you believe you deserve it.)

Having a visual and/or auditory reminder of where we are headed is an extremely powerful resource, because it gives our brain a sense of direction, and our spirit a sense of purpose.

Once you have defined your Values and Vision, they can serve as a constant reminder to assist you in making decisions on a daily basis that truly serve you. From this comes confidence in your ability to create the life you dream of.

BECOME COMFORTABLE WITH YOUR VISION FOR THE FUTURE

In Chapter Seven I talked about doing a Beliefs Audit to develop your awareness around what beliefs are running your life right now.

Recently I attended a conference called GIFTED and Lee Milteer (who was one of the speakers) shared a wonderful story about making money her friend. She told us how she went to the bank and withdrew ten thousand dollars in one hundred dollar bills and proceeded to go home and play with the money in her lounge room You heard correctly. She stuffed some down her bra, she threw it in the air and played with it.

By doing so, she sent a very clear message to the universe that she loved being abundant. That it brought her joy and that money was her friend.

You can use all the strategies in this book and have a strong desire to create an abundant life. However if deep down you have a "Poverty Consciousness" you'll never create what you desire until you do the work and release that limiting belief.

If you grew up in a very religious family and was taught that money or sex was evil you aren't about to create a lot of money in your life or have a great sex life? Or if you were brought up in a very creative household where your family did what they loved but got paid a pittance for it, you aren't likely to feel comfortable earning lots of money either.

Its really important that you understand the impact that your limiting beliefs have on your ability to create the life of your dreams. As I mentioned earlier its like weeding your emotional garden.

So before you read any further please make sure you've completed the exercises in Chapter Seven. Do your Beliefs and Behaviours Audit and once you've identified your limiting beliefs, do some sort of a ritual to release your limiting beliefs for good. Then affirm what you now believe. And repeat those new beliefs over and over every morning and every night. Either say it out loud or in your head, write it down, sing it. Whatever works best for you. And have fun creating new neural pathways.

TRACK HOW YOU'RE SPENDING YOUR TIME

Most of us seem to lead very busy lives these days, but in all that busyness, are you utilizing your time to your advantage?

BECOME YOUR #1 FAN

For the next week, just notice how you are spending your time. You might like to keep a small notepad with you and track the time you spend doing each activity.

Are you making decisions and spending your time on things that will have an optimal impact on your life? Or are some of the choices you are making "time wasters"? Facebook and Social Media Sites are wonderful but they can also become great distractions. I've certainly found myself totally losing track of time, so now I set a time limit of how long I plan to spend on them. And I set an alarm to remind me its time to log out.

Take the time to organize your time. I know it sounds obvious, but so many of us don't. We just get up and go on automatic pilot, week in, week out. I highly recommend you practice making decisions that really support your values and vision.

A word of warning, sometimes when we get clear on what we want to achieve, the universe will provide us with opportunities to really test our resolve. For example, you might have decided to lose weight and walk regularly. Next thing it rains for days on end and you get invited to lots of social outings with high carbohydrate food provided.

Instead of sabotaging your goal, take a breath and see it for what it is. An opportunity to see how committed you really are! What could you do to support your outcomes? Perhaps you could ask yourself what other ways you could exercise versus walking? If you know in advance that the food at a social event isn't part of your eating plan, perhaps you could eat beforehand or take your own?

Also be gentle on yourself if you go off track! We are human beings not robots, so inevitably we will make mistakes. Instead of chastising yourself for it, acknowledge it, work out what you'll do differently next time, and re-commit to your outcome.

WHO WE HANG OUT WITH WE BECOME

If you have a goal to be extremely successful at something but hang around with a lot of dead beats who have no motivation to achieve anything, chances are their heavy energy is going to hold you back. Similar to having a very heavy ball and chain around your ankle that you need to drag around as you do your day. Its like that wise old saying "Birds of a feather flock together."

As I mentioned earlier we're all made up of atoms. And those atoms emit a vibrational frequency. So we send out a particular vibration and like a magnet draw people with a similar vibration into our lives.

When I wanted to become a Professional Speaker I joined the National Speakers Association of Australia. And on joining found that their annual convention was the following month, so I immediately signed up to attend. I went to every monthly chapter meeting, attended Speakers Academy, and every other course they had going and in the process met so many amazing speakers who have gone on to become some of my closest friends.

We have a mutual admiration for each other and support each other through the ups and downs of making our dreams a reality.

So if you want to be the number one sales person on your team, or make the best selling authors list on amazon.com, or whatever your goal may be; find out where people that have already achieved those type of results spend their time. What conferences and conventions do they go to? Are there social media platforms that they interact on? Do they write Blogs? Is there a Linked In Group specifically for their genre?

And be brave. Often people hold back on approaching someone that has "made good" in their industry for fear of how they'll be received. Fear of being rejected, fear of looking silly, ultimately feeling unworthy of the person's time.

How do I know this? Because I've done it myself. We tend to put people that have been extremely successful on a pedestal and feel that they're living their lives on a totally different playing field. And they are! But the really cool thing is that most successful people will happily share with you what they wished they'd known when they were starting out. The pitfalls, the things they did that worked, useful resources etc. You just need to stop idolising them and realise they're human beings just like you and I. They eat, they sleep, they go to the toilet etc. And chances are if you approach them in a respectful way they'll welcome the opportunity to share what they've learnt along the way.

WE ARE IN CHARGE OF THE ENVIRONMENT WE CREATE

In his book "Hidden Messages in Water" Dr. Masuro Emoto demonstrates the power that thought has in influencing our environment. In a series of demonstrations Dr. Emoto took 50 samples of water from the same source and froze them for three hours. At -5 degrees Celsius he photographed the frozen crystals through a microscope. He then repeated the same experiment only this time the water had been exposed to various stimuli like music, words and prayer. And what he discovered was that music by Beethoven, prayer and words such as 'love" and 'thank you' taped to the sample produced beautiful intricate and perfectly symmetrical crystals. Heavy music and phrases like "you make me sick" and "I will kill you" distorted and malformed the crystals.

While Dr. Emoto's experiments are highly controversial, we all know that we can sense the energy of others without them ever opening their mouths. We've all walked into a room and sensed tension or conflict. Or walked into a room and felt a sense of excitement or positive anticipation.

When I ran my school of performing arts we would sometimes need relief teachers to cover classes for teachers that were sick or on holiday. And without fail the first time a new relief teacher took a class they would tell me how much they'd enjoyed teaching at my school. They'd say things like "the kids are different here, everyone respects each other and the students are genuinely excited about learning."

I took this compliment as a sign that we were breathing life into our Mission Statement which was, "To provide an environment where students and teachers alike could develop to their true potential." All of our team were committed to creating that environment and people literally felt it as they walked into our studio.

COLLABORATION AND TEAMWORK IS THE NAME OF THE GAME

If you ask anyone who's ever achieved anything worth while, they'll tell you that they couldn't have done it without the support of the people around them.

In my case I knew I needed other brilliant teachers to make my performing arts school the best it could be. I also needed systems in place along with fabulous administrative staff. And I needed the support of all the parents. They were all a part of my team.

Whether we consider ourselves a team player or not, all the people around us are part of our team.

- Our family
- Our friends
- Our colleagues, work mates, etc.

And once we tap into the power of the team we feel energised knowing others can cover for us and that they have our back. I don't care who you are or what you're aiming to achieve. No one can take the helm and be in charge 24 hours a day 7 days a week. Historically we know this. Historically communities or tribes have been the basis of human existence.

We've all heard of the ancient African Proverb, "It takes a village to raise a child."

And in the same vein I believe it takes a tribe to do anything worth while. Whether if it's a work tribe, a family tribe, a friendship tribe. Who's in your tribe? And do they help or hinder you? Do they have your back? Can you rely on them to be there for you when things aren't going as planned? And can they rely on you to be there for them no matter what?

A few years ago I was approached by my daughter's basketball club to come in and run some Peak Performance Coaching Sessions for their Youth League Women's Team (the Under 21s). At the time they were getting their butts whipped badly and coming 5th on the Ladder. They had never won the State League and I could tell they'd put themselves in a box and lacked the self belief and team belief that they could do so.

So we set to work releasing all their limiting beliefs based on their past performances. They learnt how to re-program their negative self talk, anchor in their wins, and instantly release any disempowering emotions after missing a basket or throwing the ball out of bounds etc, so that they could be 100 percent present on the court. They learnt the power of visualising, and writing their script and they developed a strong trust in each other's ability to never ever give up. And it started to show up in the way they were now playing.

Before each game I would spend ten minutes ensuring they were in a Peak Mental State, setting off their Positive Anchors. Their team chant became "you can rely on me to play better than I've ever played, to intercept the ball better than ever before, and shoot baskets and free throws with pin point accuracy." And sure enough they started winning all their matches.

As you can imagine the team were beside themselves with joy when they made it to the grand finals. Something they'd never achieved before. As the big day approached I knew this would be their biggest test. They had the skill, they'd developed the mental toughness and belief in each other, but did they believe deep down that they deserved to win the State Championship?

It was an amazing game. Talk about excitement plus. It was neck and neck, all the way through although they were a few points ahead for most of the match. Then as the final whistle blew the opposing team scored to make it a draw. Oh my goodness, talk about down to the wire! So the game went into extra time. Again I asked them "how bad do you want this?" I told them it was theirs for the taking. And thankfully they believed me and won!

Success is an amazing thing. It's a brilliant breeding ground to create more success. Once we've created new neural pathways in our brains, and anchored our successes in, it creates a strong foundation, or spring board to catapult us forward to the next success. And collaborating with others and achieving things as a team is by far the most powerful way to achieve anything in life.

This clever piece of prose written in 1972 by Dr. Robert

McNeish of Baltimore takes certain migration charac-
teristics of geese and applies the concepts to human
behavior and teamwork. It provides a perfect example
of the importance of team work and how it can have a
profound and powerful effect on any form of personal
or business endeavor.

When we use these five principles in our personal and
business life it will help us to foster and encourage a level
of passion and energy in ourselves, as well as those who
are our friends, associates or team members.

It is essential to remember that teamwork happens
inside and outside of business life when it is continually
nurtured and encouraged.

LESSONS FROM GEESE

Lesson 1 - The Importance of Achieving Goals

As each goose flaps its wings it creates an UPLIFT
for the birds that follow. By flying in a 'V' formation the
whole flock adds 71 percent extra to the flying range.

Outcome

When we have a sense of community and focus, we
create trust and can help each other to achieve our goals.

Lesson 2 - The Importance of Team Work

When a goose falls out of formation it suddenly feels

the drag and resistance of flying alone. It quickly moves back to take advantage of the lifting power of the birds in front.

Outcome

If we had as much sense as geese we would stay in formation with those headed where we want to go. We are willing to accept their help and give our help to others.

Lesson 3 - The Importance of Sharing

When a goose tires of flying up front it drops back into formation and another goose flies to the point position.

Outcome

It pays to take turns doing the hard tasks. We should respect and protect each other's unique arrangement of skills, capabilities, talents and resources.

Lesson 4 - The Importance of Empathy and Understanding

When a goose gets sick, two geese drop out of formation and follow it down to the ground to help and protect it.

Outcome

If we have as much sense as geese we will stand by each other in difficult times, as well as when we are strong.

Lesson 5 - The Importance of Encouragement

Geese flying in formation 'HONK' to encourage those up front to keep up with their speed.

Outcome

We need to make sure our honking is encouraging. In groups and teams where there is encouragement, production is much greater. 'Individual empowerment results from quality honking'

Here's a link to see a beautiful video presentation of Lessons from Geese on my website:

http://www.theconfidencecoach.net.au/resources/a-touch-of-inspiration/

BIGGEST NIGHTMARE OR BIGGEST GIFT?

Let's face it, life will throw you some curve balls on your way to creating the life of your dreams. Sometimes as a test to see if you really want it, and other times providing the necessary steps in your growth to become who you've been placed on this earth to become.

In my case I needed to go through that incredibly dark time in my early thirties to become the women I am today. I believe we all come here with a purpose. And I know that my Life Purpose is all about lighting people up to believe in themselves and their capabilities. And while I'd always enjoyed inspiring people I didn't have the knowledge, skills or ability to do that 25 years ago. So life threw me a curve ball that took me on a journey to rediscover who I really was, and what I was meant to be doing with my life.

In my darkest hour I felt as though I was living in a nightmare, but when I chose life, and pulled myself out of that big black hole I realised that life had presented me with my biggest gift. The opportunity to create a brand new version of who I wanted to become.

My dear friend and speaking buddy Sam Cawthorn is a classic example of turning his biggest nightmare into his biggest gift.

In October 2006 Sam's life changed forever when he was involved in a major car accident, where he was pronounced DEAD. He was thankfully resuscitated, but left with an amputated right arm and a permanent disability in his right leg.

Sam was hospitalized for over five months and was told that he may not survive and best case was that if he was to survive he would never walk again. A year later he defied all odds taking his first steps into a new life, where his story would continue to inspire and change the lives of Australians and people all over the world.

However as Sam states in his book Bounce Forward ~ How to Turn Crisis into Success, "before his accident he had no compelling purpose in life. He had forgotten his "why" or perhaps had never really known it."

Sam saw his accident as a major wake up call. And he certainly answered the call. These days he's a busy global keynote speaker sharing the stage with the likes of the Dalai Lama, Steve Wozniak and Brian Tracy. He is also a successful businessman and philanthropist.

BOUNCE FOWARD

I love Sam's twist on the well known phrase Bounce Back. If we bounce back to where and who we were before life threw us a curve ball, we aren't taking the lessons we've learnt with us. And let's face it, often times we can't go back to being that person because we've changed; either physically like Sam or in my case, emotionally.

These days when things don't turn out the way I'd planned I put all my attention on looking for the gift in the situation. The sooner I see the gift, the sooner I'm able to adjust my sails, change my emotional state and choose a different course of action.

CHAPTER ELEVEN

Rituals to Create the Life of Your Dreams

As I mentioned previously, before we even get out of bed we can put ourselves in a Peak Performance State. Unfortunately, we can also do the exact opposite.

For example, if someone is working in a job that they don't like, it's highly likely they'll hit the snooze button on their alarm, lay there until they really have to get up, and then have to race around like crazy to be out the door on time to go to work. Chances are their internal dialogue is working overtime saying incredibly disempowering things which then impacts their physiology and their ability to function efficiently, and ultimately impact what kind of day they're going to have.

Imagine instead waking up feeling excited about your life. Feeling energised and busting to get out of bed to start your day. And before getting out of bed you read your daily affirmation that goes like this:

DAILY AFFIRMATION

Every morning, I awaken centred, strong, happy, full of love and confidence, faith and joy. I am peaceful, full of vigour and life and ready to take on and complete with AMAZING SUCCESS anything that is put in front, behind or anywhere near my sphere of influence!

Every day I grow stronger and stronger in my faith and my ability. There is a clean, clear window in which to see the glorious future that is my birthright!

I wake up grateful and full of positive love and calmness. I am as calm and comfortable as a placid pond early on a warm spring dawn, and I remain that way throughout the day and into the night, where I feel even more of the positive feelings and emotions that make me function at my very best!

God's gift of prosperity continues to flow freely to me, in oceans of glorious abundance, confidence, focus and health, and wealth beyond my wildest dreams. And I am grateful beyond measure as I continue to create even more health, wealth, happiness and joy for all that I have the privilege of meeting and touching.

All of these things are here in my life right here, right now, and I experience them even more with each and every breath I take. I am LOVE, I give LOVE and I receive LOVE from myself and all that are in my life.

What sort of day do you think you'll have if you start it by saying something similar to yourself? I never get out of bed without saying this affirmation. Its how I start every day.

And it has a huge impact on how I feel. Remember the meaning we give to something causes an emotion, that emotion/feeling drives a particular behaviour and that behaviour produces a result. So if we want to create a different outcome or result, it all starts with the meaning we give to something.

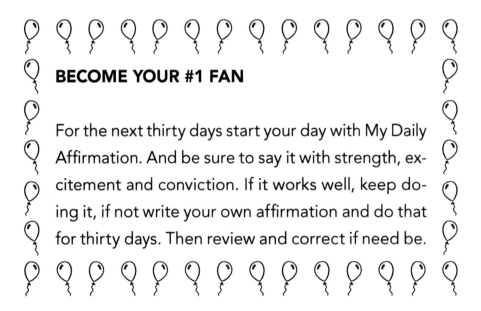

BECOME YOUR #1 FAN

For the next thirty days start your day with My Daily Affirmation. And be sure to say it with strength, excitement and conviction. If it works well, keep doing it, if not write your own affirmation and do that for thirty days. Then review and correct if need be.

At the moment I'm reading a brilliant book by Pam Grout. It's called E Squared ~ Nine Do it Yourself Energy Experiments That Prove Your Thoughts Create Your Reality.

I highly recommend you buy yourself a copy. Here's the link: http://pamgrout.com/e-squared/

ARE YOU A HUMAN BEING OR A HUMAN DOING?

Do you ever find yourself wishing there was another day in the week to stop, take a breath and relax? Sometimes I joke and suggest that we should add a new day in the week called Sumunday – the day between Sunday and Monday. That way we could all do everything we normally do, and still have one day up our sleeves to sit back and relax. My guess is that we would still manage to fill that day with lots of things to do! Which brings me to my point. We've lost touch with how to "be" because we are all so busy "doing."

> *"It is important from time to time to slow down, to go away by yourself, and simply be." ~ Eileen Caddy*

Taking the time to just "be" can be an extremely valuable way to connect with who we really are.

THE POWER OF MEDITATION

Researchers speculate that primitive hunter-gatherer societies may have discovered meditation and its altered states of consciousness while staring at the flames of their fires. Over thousands of years, meditation evolved into a structured practice. Indian scriptures called "tantras" mentioned meditation techniques 5000 years ago.

Buddha, one of history's major proponents of meditation, and a major meditation icon, first made his mark around 500 B.C. His teachings were spread far and wide across the Asian continent. Separate countries or cultures adopted different forms of the word "meditation," and they each found their own unique way of practicing it. Buddhist and Hindu-based Eastern-style meditation practices are still the most popular today.

Meditation was spread to Western society thousands of years after it was developed in the East.

It finally started to gain popularity in the West in the mid-20th century. In the 1960s and 1970s, many professors and researchers began testing the effects of meditation and learned about its multitude of benefits. Meditation can be a great way to add balance to our busy lives. Many years ago I certainly benefited greatly from learning to do Transcendental Meditation.

And these days even the medical profession is aware of the benefits of meditation.

It's a piece of advice yogis have given for thousands of years, take a deep breath and relax. Watch the tension melt from your muscles and all your niggling worries vanish. Somehow we all know that relaxation is good for us.

A recent publication reports that researchers at Harvard Medical School discovered, in long-term practitioners of relaxation methods such as yoga and meditation, far more "disease-fighting genes" were active, compared to those who practised no form of relaxation.

In particular, they found genes that protect from disorders such as pain, infertility, high blood pressure and even rheumatoid arthritis were switched on. The changes, say the researchers, were induced by what they call "the relaxation effect", a phenomenon that could be just as powerful as any medical drug but without the side effects. "We found a range of disease-fighting genes were active in the relaxation practitioners that were not active in the control group," said lead researcher, Dr Herbert Benson, Associate Professor of Medicine at Harvard Medical School. The good news for the control group with the less-healthy genes is that the research didn't stop there.

The experiment, which showed just how responsive genes are to behaviour, mood and environment, revealed that genes can switch on, just as easily as they switch off. "Harvard researchers asked the control group to start practising relaxation methods every day," said Jake Toby, hypnotherapist at London's BodyMind Medicine Centre. Toby went on to say, "After two months, their bodies began to change, the genes that help fight inflammation, kill diseased cells and protect the body from cancer all began to switch on."

More encouraging still, the benefits of the relaxation

effect were found to increase with regular practice; the more people practised relaxation methods such as meditation or deep breathing, the greater their chances of remaining free of arthritis and joint pain with stronger immunity, healthier hormone levels and lower blood pressure. Benson believes the research is pivotal because it shows how a person's state of mind affects the body on a physical and genetic level. It might also explain why relaxation induced by meditation or repetitive mantras is considered to be a powerful remedy in traditions such as Ayurveda in Indian or Tibetan medicine.

But just how can relaxation have such wide-ranging and powerful effects? Research has described the negative effects of stress on the body. Linked to the release of the stress-hormones adrenalin and cortisol, stress raises the heart rate and blood pressure, weakens immunity and lowers fertility. By contrast, the state of relaxation is linked to higher levels of feel-good chemicals such as serotonin and to the growth hormone which repairs cells and tissue. Indeed, studies show that relaxation has virtually the opposite effect, lowering heart rate, boosting immunity and enabling the body to thrive.

"On a biological level, stress is linked to fight-flight and danger," said Dr. Jane Flemming, a London GP. "In survival mode, heart rate rises and blood pressure shoots up. Meanwhile muscles, preparing for danger, contract and tighten. And non-essential functions such as immunity and digestion go by the wayside."Relaxation, on the other hand, is a state of rest, enjoyment and physical renewal. Free of danger, muscles can relax and food can be digested. The heart can slow and blood circulation flows freely to the body's tissues, feeding it with nutrients and oxygen. This restful state is good for fertility, as the body is able to conserve the resources it needs to generate new life.

While relaxation techniques can be very different, their biological effects are essentially similar. "When you relax, the parasympathetic nervous system switches on. That is linked to better digestion, memory and immunity, among other things," said Toby. "As long as you relax deeply, you'll reap the rewards." But, he warns, deep relaxation isn't the sort of switching off you do relaxing with a cup of tea or lounging on the sofa.

"What you're looking for is a state of deep relaxation where tension is released from the body on a physical level and your mind completely switches off," he said. "The effect won't be achieved by lounging round in an everyday way, nor can you force yourself to relax. You can only really achieve it by learning a specific technique such as self-hypnosis, guided imagery or meditation."

The relaxation effect, however, may not be as pronounced on everyone. "Some people are more susceptible to relaxation methods than others," said Joan Borysenko, director of a relaxation program for outpatients at Beth Israel Deaconess Medical Centre in Boston. "Through relaxation, we find some people experience a little improvement, others a lot. And there are a few whose lives turn around totally."

SEVEN HEALTH BENEFITS OF DEEP RELAXATION

The next time you tune out and switch off and let yourself melt, remind yourself of all the good work the relaxation effect is doing on your body. These are just some of the scientifically proven benefits.

1. INCREASED IMMUNITY

Relaxation appears to boost immunity in recovering cancer patients. A study at the Ohio State University found that progressive muscular relaxation, when practised daily, reduced the risk of breast cancer recurrence. In another study at Ohio State, a month of relaxation exercises boosted natural killer cells in the elderly, giving them a greater resistance to tumours and to viruses.

2. EMOTIONAL BALANCE

Emotional balance, means to be free of all the neurotic behaviour that results from the existence of a tortured and traumatised ego. This is very hard to achieve fully, but meditation certainly is the way to cure such neurosis and unhealthy emotional states. As one's consciousness is cleansed of emotionally soaked memories, not only does great freedom abound, but also great balance. As one's responses then are not coloured by the burdens one carries, but are instead true, direct and appropriate.

3. INCREASED FERTILITY

A study at the University of Western Australia found that women are more likely to conceive during periods when they are relaxed rather than stressed. A study at Trakya University, in Turkey, also found that stress reduces sperm count and motility, suggesting relaxation may also boost male fertility.

4. RELIEVES IRRITABLE BOWEL SYNDROME

When patients suffering from irritable bowel syndrome began practising a relaxation meditation twice daily, their symptoms of bloating, diarrhoea and constipation improved significantly. The meditation was so effective the researchers at the State University of New York recommended it as an effective treatment.

5. LOWERS BLOOD PRESSURE

A study at Harvard Medical School found that meditation lowered blood pressure by making the body less responsive to stress hormones, in a similar way to blood pressure-lowering medication. Meanwhile a British Medical Journal report found that patients trained how to relax had significantly lower blood pressure.

6. ANTI-INFLAMATORY

Stress leads to inflammation, a state linked to heart disease, arthritis, asthma and skin conditions such as psoriasis. According to researchers at Emory University, relaxation can help prevent and treat such symptoms by switching off the stress response. In this way, one study at McGill University found that meditation clinically improved the symptoms of psoriasis.

7. CALMNESS

The simple difference between those who meditate and those who do not, is that for a meditative mind the thought occurs but is witnessed, while for an ordinary mind, the thought occurs and is the boss. So in both minds, an upsetting thought can occur, but for those who meditate it is just another thought, which is seen as such and is allowed to blossom and die, while in the ordinary mind the thought instigates a storm which rages on and on.

How to switch off stress: How can you use relaxation's healing powers?

Harvard researchers found that yoga, meditation and even repetitive prayer and mantras all induced the relaxation effect. "The more regularly these techniques are practised, the more deeply rooted the benefits will be," said Toby. Try one or more of these techniques for 15 minutes once or twice a day.

Body Scan

Starting with your head and working down to your arms and feet, notice how you feel in your body. Taking in your head and neck, simply notice if you feel tense, relaxed, calm or anxious. See how much you can spread any sensations of softness and relaxation to areas of your body that feel tense. Once your reach your feet, work back up your body.

Breath Focus

Sit comfortably. Tune into your breath, follow the sensation of inhaling from your nose to abdomen and out again. Let tension go with each exhalation. When you notice your mind wandering, return to your breath.

Mantra Repetition

The relaxation response can be evoked by sitting quietly with eyes closed for 15 minutes twice a day, and mentally repeating a simple word or sound such as "Om."

Guided Imagery

Imagine a wonderfully relaxing light or a soothing waterfall washing away tension from your body and mind. Make your image vivid, imagining texture, colour and any fragrance as the image washes over you.

If you're a total novice you may find guided visualisation is a great place to start. There are a lot of different CDs available. One of my favourite ones is called *Rainforest*. The person's voice would take me on a journey into a lush green rainforest and for ten or twenty minutes (depending on how much time I had) I would escape from the stresses of my day to day life into the lush green rainforest setting, complete with a beautiful rock pool and waterfall.

You'll also find one on my Audio Book "Positive ways to Transform your Day." It's called "Your Special Place." It's under 8 mins and lets face it we can all manage to find eight minutes in our day to stop, connect with our spirit and rejuvenate.

You can download YOUR FREE COPY here:

http://www.theconfidencecoach.net.au/resources/relaxation-and-visualisation/

Sometimes we can slot in small moments of tranquillity to our day. My favourite way to start my day is to make myself a cup of chai tea and sit on our swinging seat by the pool and gaze out to sea. The suburb we live in has breathtaking views of the ocean and lots of palm trees and birdlife, so I treasure those five to ten minutes that I spend each morning just sitting listening to the birds and drinking in my lush green surroundings.

For those of you that are saying, "well that's all well and good for you, but I can't do that where I live." I suggest you get creative and keep your eye out for a spot. It might be a park that you walk past on the way to the bus? Or a brisk walk at lunchtime to find a peaceful spot to eat your lunch and just relax?

And if none of those options are available to you, you can download an App to your computer, smart phone or iPad. My teenage daughter found a free App on Calm. com that is beautiful. Once you download the App you can choose from approximately sixteen different scenes that all come with a guided relaxation and the sounds of nature.

I'm not very scientifically inclined, however I do know that all living things are made up of atoms of energy. So by surrounding ourselves by nature, we can't help but feel the benefits. Sometimes if I'm feeling sad, or depleted of energy I'll find a tree trunk with soft bark and wrap my arms around it. Now, I know some of you are saying, "are you for real???" But don't knock it until you've tried it! Tree trunks that are large enough to hug have been around for a very long time and have a beautiful energy that emanates from them. Another way I ground myself is to walk bare foot on soft green grass, or walk along a soft sandy beach.

It always brings my focus right into present time, (versus racing ahead in my mind) and every time, without fail, I come away from the experience feeling calmer, grounded and more able to connect with my loved ones from a peaceful space.

Another wonderful way to give yourself the gift of peace and tranquillity is to take yourself off to your own "Special Place". Just like the one on my Audio Book.

Put on some soft relaxation music (without words) and find a comfortable place to sit where you won't be disturbed. Turn off mobile phones etc., sit down, close your eyes and just focus on your breathing. Allow your breath to find its natural rhythm and do your best to empty your mind of any thoughts. If you notice your mind taking you off on a tangent, just notice it and bring yourself back to focusing on your breath. Once you feel relaxed (only you will be able to determine when that is) take yourself off to a beautiful tranquil setting.

It might be near the water, it might be in a beautiful valley, or snow capped mountain, or it may even be floating on a beautiful soft cloud. Use your imagination to create your own "Special Place".

For some of you, you'll see a clear picture, others may see a fuzzy picture but get a strong sense of how it feels, while others may get a fuzzy sense of how it looks and feels, but be able to hear clearly the various sounds that surround you. Spend as little or as long as you like, drinking in the sensations that come with being in your special place and feeling this relaxed.

Some of you might be wondering what being relaxed has to do with developing your self esteem and self confidence? And that's a great question!

As I mentioned earlier, we can get caught up doing our lives like a mouse on a wheel. Running in circles on automatic pilot, and getting nowhere! Taking the time to give yourself the gift of solitude, can be a wonderful way to connect with your innermost thoughts and desires. It's amazing how clear we can get on what's important to us, when we take the time to step back and ponder.

SCRIPT WRITING

The power of the written word is highly under rated. Getting goals and outcomes out of our head and onto paper, even when it feels like a pipe dream or something beyond your reach is incredibly powerful.

THE POWER OF THE WRITTEN WORD

I came across this beautiful letter recently from one of my gorgeous students that I'd taken to see Cinderella.

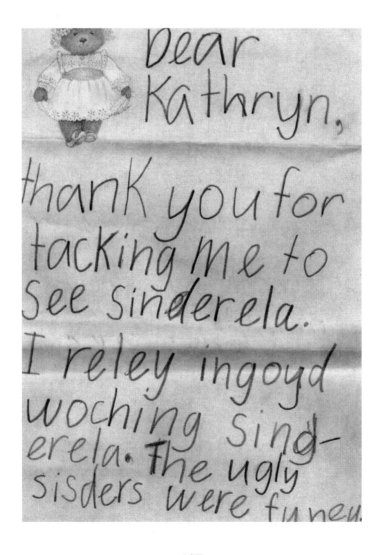

Dear Kathryn,

thank you for tacking me to see sinderela. I reley ingoyd woching sinderela. The ugly sisders were funeu.

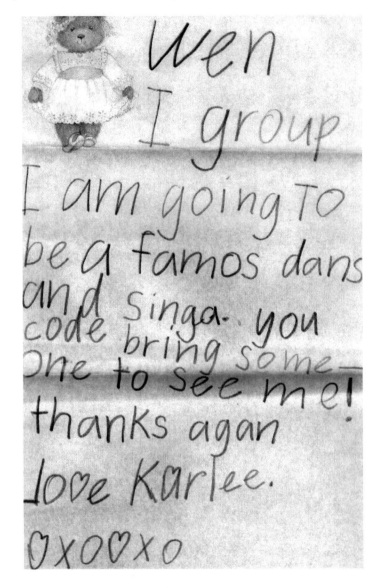

Wen
I group
I am going To
be a famos dans
and singa. you
code bring some
one to see me!
thanks agan
love Karlee.
OXOOXO

At the time that Karlee wrote me that "Thank You Note" she was about six or seven years old. And she's the client I mentioned earlier who landed one of the lead roles in A Chorus Line! Can you imagine my delight after having taught her dance from age four to fourteen and

Peak Performance Coached her as a young adult; to be sitting in the audience watching her up there living the dream that she dared to dream as a seven year old? Tears flowed down my face, and my whole body was covered in goosebumps. And not only had she landed a lead role in A Chorus Line, every single critics review had singled her out for her outstanding portrayal of Diana.

So writing Letters from the Future and Scripts can be an incredibly powerful tool.

I always get my clients to incorporate this powerful tool once they've developed self esteem, self worth and self belief about their ability to make their dreams a reality.

Recently I coached a gorgeous young woman who had failed her Physiotherapy Exam three times. If she failed it the fourth time she couldn't become accredited in the U.S. So it was do or die. To make matters worse she had just split up with her boyfriend so, she was not in the most resourceful emotional state.

Her brother is my personal trainer so he suggested that she have some sessions with me to set herself up for success this time. So we set about letting go of all of her limiting beliefs and building her self esteem, self worth and self belief. And then the next step was getting her to write her script for exactly how she wanted her exam to go. Right through to receiving the notification that she had passed. And of course she passed with flying colours.

Another client who was an aspiring opera singer had two sessions with me before flying over to New York City to audition for numerous roles in opera companies across the U.S. She had flown over the previous year and come home devastated knowing that she hadn't performed to the best of her ability, so this time she was determined to make amends.

In the two coaching sessions she had before she left we uncovered her sabotage pattern (which was all about playing the compare and despair game) which left her feeling inadequate. So often in life we compare ourselves to others and wish we were like them in some way. For example as talented as them, slim as them, intelligent as them etc..... And it has a devastating affect on our self esteem. In my clients case, we tracked back to the first time she had felt inadequate. It was when she had been studying to be an opera singer. Her best friend always got the roles that she had wanted. So she started to believe that she wasn't talented enough and didn't deserve them. Once we identified where her limiting beliefs came from we proceeded to collapse those negative anchors once and for all. And then moved on to set her up for success. With her Circle of Excellence well and truly anchored in she headed home to write her script for exactly how she wanted her auditions to unfold.

I remember getting goosebumps when I opened her email to tell me that not only were her auditions going exactly as she had written in her script, her agent's wife (who was the top vocal coach in the U.S. with a huge waiting list of clients wanting to be coached by her) had agreed to coach her.

In the process of being coached by her, my client had a dream. In the dream she and her vocal coach were in a sacred building, something like a church, and her coach handed her a beautiful wooden box with a gift inside it. The famous opera singer, Placido Domingo, was there in the building too. Before my client got to open the wooden box she woke up.

The next day as she was about to leave her voice lesson her coach gave her a complimentary ticket to the Metropolitan Opera Company's Performance. Immediately she connected the dots from her dream. This was the gift that she had dreamt about. But the gift didn't end there. When she arrived to watch the performance she found she was sitting next to a fellow soprano that was studying with the Metropolitan Opera Company. And she invited her backstage to meet the cast. My client graciously accepted her offer and couldn't believe her eyes. As they walked backstage guess who the first person she got to meet was? The man himself, Placido Domingo.

And to finish the story, my client came home with two contracts to perform in operas in the U.S. News travels fast in the world of opera. So on arriving back to Australia she also got booked to perform in two australian companies. And the role she landed in both companies was none other than the one her friend had always been cast in as a teenager. Queen of the Night in The Magic Flute, which is known to have one of the hardest aria's of all the operas.

Not only are the two arias very complex to sing, they are completely different in style; "The first aria calls for a lyrical and flexible voice, while the second requires a dramatic and powerful voice. My client told me that often opera buffs go to The Magic Flute just to see if the Soprano can pull of the arias.

Since then my client returned to her homeland of Hungary and is still performing and living her dream! Here's a video of her singing the aria in question.

http://www.youtube.com/watch?v=oEJ2kl75PVM

I could share so many more stories of clients writing scripts and having not only that but other amazing things they could never have imagined unfold before their eyes. Its a very powerful process. And remember the key is really believing that you deserve it!

TIPS IN WRITING YOUR SCRIPT

- Use what Tony Robbins refers to as Transformational Vocabulary. In other words, juicy words that pump you up and create a can-do feeling and a fire in your belly. Words like effortlessly, easily, magically etc.

- Write it in past tense as if it's already happened. Our brains don't know the difference between fiction and reality, so telling your brain it has already happened is a bit like turning on the GPS in your brain and telling it where to go and what to create.

- Be sure to follow through to your desired outcome and what it's given you. What evidence will you have when you've achieved it?

VISUALISE YOUR WAY TO SUCCESS

Visualising is another incredibly powerful tool.

The great golfer Jack Nicklaus said, "I never hit a shot, not even in practice, without having a very sharp, in-focus picture of it in my head. First I see the ball where I want it to finish, nice and white and sitting up high on the bright green grass. Then the scene quickly changes, and I see the ball going there; its path, trajectory, and shape, even its behavior on landing. Then there is a sort of fade-out, and the next scene shows me making the kind of swing that will turn the previous images into reality."

According to TIME magazine, on the night before the 1984 finals in women's gymnastics, Mary Lou Retton, then

16, laid in bed at the Olympic Village mentally rehearsing. A believer in the process of mental conditioning and affirmation, she had done the same hundreds of times. Night after night, she visualised herself performing her routines perfectly. In her mind, she saw every move, she rehearsed every move mentally, again and again. The result? A performance of perfection, charm and confidence, culminating in the sixteen year old winning an Olympic gold medal.

Athletes in all sports are taught to visualise perfect performances in advance of the event. This is because the mind and nervous system can't tell the difference between a real event and a vividly imagined event.

Proof of this is in your dreaming. How many times have you had a dream when it seemed just as real to you as your awake state?

At the U.S. Olympic training center, athletes were hooked up to monitors and told to visualise and then to actually perform. It turns out that the same neural networks get fired.

Between 1956 – 1980, Russia was untouchable in gymnastics. Larissa Latynina, Nikolai Andrianov and Boris Shakhlin were at the core of the Russian Gymnastic's golden years. Larissa won an amazing nine gold medals, while Nikolai and Boris each won seven, cementing their places amongst the all time great Olympians.

During those Golden years for the Russians, nobody

could argue about their performance. They won because they were simply better. They executed their routines to perfection. They were awesome. But one question was always on everyone's mind, "How did they manage to execute their routines perfectly all the time, if not most of the time?"

It was only in the late 1980s that **the secret was finally uncovered.**

The Russians had employed the use of mental imagery training, what we now affectionately termed as visualisation. They would not only train physically, but they would also mentally rehearse their routines hundreds of times before the actual competition.

The Russians had discovered a revolutionary way of improving sports performance!

There was a study conducted by Dr. Blaslotto at the University Of Chicago to determine the effects of visualisation on performance. Dr. Blaslotto would gather a group of basketball players, and set out to test how visualisation training would impact a player's performance.

The performance measure would be the selected basketball players' free throw percentage. For fairness, he would randomly assign the athletes to one of three groups, and he would take their free throw percentage before starting the experiment.

The first group would go to the gym and practice making free throws everyday for one hour.

The second group also would go to the gym. But instead of picking up a basketball and shooting, they would lie on the ground and spend their time visualising themselves making successful free throws.

The third group was the control, and they did not do anything.

30 days later, the three groups were retested.

The Results:

As expected, the third group did not show any improvement.

The first group of players, who had physically practiced, improved their free throw percentage by 24%.

What was truly amazing was that the second group, who did not physically make a single free throw, actually improved their free throw percentage by 23%! Just one percentage lower than those who practiced everyday for one hour!

Visualisation can DOUBLE your progress! And you don't have to be an athlete to use it! People like you and I can get the same amazing results.

Reference: http://www.hypnosisrelease.com/Sports-Hypnosis.html

The other day in my session with my Personal Trainer he decided running up the flight of stairs was too easy for me so he asked me to miss every second step, then we professed to me jumping up the stairs with both feet together. Talk about upping the ante! But he knew I was up for the challenge. Before I proceeded I took a few deep breaths, closed my eyes and saw myself doing it easily, then I did my Power Move setting of my Positive Anchor and guess what? I did it! And not just once, but several reps! So this stuff works. As I said earlier, the mind and nervous system can't tell the difference between a real event and a vividly imagined event.

Here's another story that illustrates the fact that our brain has the capacity to create what we visualise and to make sure we're visualising every single detail right through to the desired result.

In 1989, I attended Robert Kiyosaki's Business School for Entrepreneurs in Hawaii. We were all put on exercise teams. And one of our tasks was to get our team as fit as possible to prepare for a team challenge on the last day. We had no idea what it was going to be, just that we needed to train every morning before breakfast and all would be revealed in due course. As it turned out we were to compete in a team triathlon. We had to choose one member of our team to do the swim leg (across a bay) and another team member to do the bike leg, followed by the whole team running, walking or crawling across the finish line for the final leg.

I was quite fit at the time so volunteered to lead the team along with my male counterpart. When we heard about our task we asked our group who would like to do the swim leg, and one of the women volunteered. She'd been a competitive swimmer in her youth and felt confident that she could do a great job. She had also trained in NLP and knew how to Future Pace i.e: Visualise the outcome she wanted. So she set about preparing for the race. When the gun went off she hit the water with steel determination, and quickly hit the lead, (even though the majority of her competitors were male). As she reached the other side of the bay she had blitzed the field.

But alas, she had only visualised making it to the other side of the bay in first place. As all the swimmers came out of the water they had to make their way up a very rocky beach. There was hardly any sand. It was virtually broken coral and shells, so it felt like she was walking across cut glass. Unfortunately, as she gingerly made her way across the rocky terrain, several swimmers ran past her. After we'd completed the challenge and we de-briefed what happened, she shared that she had only visualised getting to the other side of the bay first. So she got a great distinction; to visualise all the way to the final outcome.

So what are you waiting for? What can you start visualising today?

STACKING ANCHORS

Another way we can set ourselves up for success is to build on previous successes. And as I mentioned previously whenever we're in a heightened state (either positive or negative) we're unconsciously anchoring those states into our nervous system. And whenever something similar happens it unconsciously triggers those same emotions.

After I'd climbed out of my big black hole of depression, I couldn't understand why every year as July rolled around I would feel depressed again. Not to the level I was when I was feeling suicidal but flat and lethargic nonetheless. And then I realised the time of year was a "trigger" for me. I'd unknowingly anchored in to "feel bad" in July. Once I recognised what was happening I was able to collapse that negative anchor and replace it with a positive one. And July doesn't have that negative impact on me any more.

In my case it was a time of year that triggered my negative anchor but negative anchors can be triggered by anything, for example the music that was playing when you broke up with your ex, a particular car, someone that looks similar to someone that hurt us, or has the same name etc.

If you find you have a negative emotion that keeps on being triggered I highly recommend you find an NLP Practitioner to help you collapse the negative anchor once and for all.

And then set about stacking some Positive Anchors. Every time you have a win, no matter how small or large find a way to anchor those emotions into your body.

Its best to anchor it in just as your reach the peak

of the emotion. At that precise moment do something physical that is easy to repeat whenever you want to feel that emotion again. Be sure to make it simple so that you can do it in public. For example, you could squeeze your ear lobe, or make a fist and say yes, or create your own "power move." If you watch most elite athletes they have a power move that they do when they're doing well. Australian Tennis Star Lleyton Hewitt has a signature move that he makes with his arm when he's broken his opponents serve or won a particularly hard point. He bends his wrist and points his hand towards his head and says "c'mon" loud and with passion and intensity. Lots of soccer players will lift their shirts over their head and run when they score a goal or penalty shoot out. And what they're doing is not only celebrating but anchoring in their success. And of course the more you stack the anchors the more powerful they are.

Every time I hear the music "Eye of the Tiger" my whole physiology changes. My posture become very erect and upright, my pulse fastens, my eyes become very intense and focused and my breathing changes to a slow even rhythm. Because I've used that particular piece of music a lot to get myself into an incredibly positive focused state before demonstrating how to break a piece of board with your bare hand. So no matter how tired or scattered I'm feeling, the moment I hear that music my state automatically changes.

RESEARCH SUPPORTING THE PRINCIPLES OF ANCHORING

Of the hundreds of examples of anchoring principles applied in an innovative way, without the name "Anchoring", one stands out for me.

It is Ellen Langer's study of two groups of elderly men (aged 75-80 years), at Harvard University. For five days, these two comparable groups of men lived in a closely supervised retreat centre out in the country. One group was engaged in a series of tasks encouraging them to think about the past (to write an autobiography, to discuss the past etc). The other group was engaged in a series of tasks which actually anchored them back into a past time (1959). They wrote an autobiography only up to 1959, describing that time as "now", watched 1959 movies, had 1959 music playing on the "radios", and lived with only the artefacts available in 1951. Before and after the five days, both groups were studied on a number of criteria associated with ageing.

While the first group stayed constant or actually deteriorated on these criteria, the second group dramatically improved on physical health measures such as joint flexibility, vision, and muscle breadth, as well as on IQ tests. They were anchored back to being 50 years old, by the sights and sounds of 1959.

LISTEN TO YOUR INTUITION

In 1994, I flew to The Big Island of Hawaii to attend Anthony Robbins' Mastery University. And it was at that course that I had the privilege of meeting Deepak Chopra who was one of the Guest Speakers.

Every since I've been an avid follower of Deepak's work and love to start my day with his morning meditations. The other day I was sitting doing one of his meditations and the focus was intuition.

Now intuition is a widely used word but what exactly does it mean? In philosophy intuition is defined as instinctive knowledge or belief. Knowledge obtained neither by reason nor perception.

Deepak describes it as, "A sacred message obtained directly from the source of all knowledge, the mind of nature, the cosmic computer. Universal intelligence and the part of our body that is most receptive to intuition is the heart."

So that well known phrase "follow your heart" carries the ultimate truth.

Have you ever dismissed a sense of intuition only to realise it would have served you more to listen to it? I know I have. And kicked myself after the fact for not taking notice.

Or on the other hand, have you ever been drawn to do something even though your logical mind is flexing its muscles and trying to persuade you not to? Deepak teaches we all have that inner voice inside of us that can give us the answers, its the ability to connect with some type of great knowledge. But often we choose not to or fail to hear our inner voice's wisdom.

Two things that can cloud ones' intuition are fear and desire. If you quiet your mind and come to that stillness within that is beyond fear or desire you will find your source of pure intuition. Our "intuitive heart" is where we can connect with our "essence" and manifesting power.

In November 2011, I had the opportunity to attend a women's conference in LA and welcome in and celebrate 11.11.11. So I went ahead and booked in to the conference. And just before I booked my return flights to Sydney I thought "what the heck, why don't I break my trip up on the way home and stop off in Hawaii for a week or so to catch up with friends, have a much needed rest and finish writing my book?" And so I did.

I was up on North Shore for my birthday which also happened to be Thanksgiving. So after spending the morning with a friend I ventured out of the resort to explore the area. The beauty that surrounded me took my breathe away. So before I knew it my walk had spontaneously turned into a "walking meditation."

I made my way through the rainforest and as I stepped out onto the beach the first thing I saw was a half a coconut shell in the shape of a heart sitting on the sand directly in front of me. I immediately knew it was a "gift" for me, so reached down, picked it up and thanked Mother Nature for her beautiful birthday gift.

Then within seconds of picking up my gift a poem started coming out of my mouth. And it went like this:

Listen to the waves as they crash upon the shore;
listen if you will as you open the door.
The door to your heart, your dreams and desires.
Let your spirit guides guide you along the way,
make your dreams happen come what may.

I placed my beautiful coconut shell on a rock and proceeded to record the poem and put it on Facebook to inspire my friends. But is often the case the message was really for me.

You see when I got home to Australia I felt like a fish out of water, and realised that my heart had been calling me to Hawaii for years. And it was finally time to answer the call.

Long story short we packed up our belongings, rented out our home in Sydney and flew in to start our new lives here in Honolulu on 15th March 2013. And I can honestly say I've never been happier.

So what does your Intuitive Heart say to you? And are you listening?

Click here to see a picture of my beautiful coconut shell and read the Blog I wrote about it:

http://www.theconfidencecoach.net.au/do-you-listen-to-your-intuition/#sthash.9lo3KK6i.dpuf

THE POWER OF GRATITUDE

By starting our day with focusing on what we're grateful for, we set the tone for the rest of our day. Where our attention goes our energy flows! We've all heard the saying, Is your glass half empty of half full? Meaning what do you focus on in life? What you haven't got, or what you have got?

It's a Universal Law that what we focus on, shows up in our lives. I remember many years ago my first dance teacher saying to me, "You're so lucky, you always seem to fall on your feet". What she was referring to was that amazing opportunities seemed to show up in my life on a regular basis.

Now back then, I hadn't studied any personal development, however, I did have a happy disposition, and was known for my "Pollyanna" outlook on life. In other words, I would always be able to find something positive in every situation. For example, if a friend had broken their arm, and it wasn't their dominant arm, I'd reassure them and say how lucky they were, because they could still eat, write, dress themselves etc. If they'd broken their dominant arm, I would say it was a wonderful opportunity to become ambidextrous.

A few years ago my daughter had a friend at school in Grade 6 that tended to spend a lot of her day in what we refer to as "Vixen the Victim Mode." She spent her day complaining and moaning about what her and her family didn't have. It drove my daughter absolutely insane, because I've brought her up with the exact opposite perspective. So when her friend was complaining about not liking her lunch and that she was starving, my daughter quickly pointed out that people in Ethiopia and other third world countries really were starving and that it might be more useful to be grateful for what she has got ie; a roof over her head and three meals a day (even if it wasn't the food she would prefer)

So what are you grateful for?

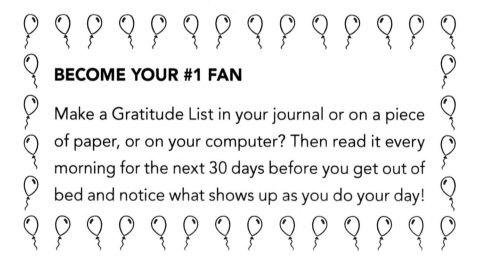

BECOME YOUR #1 FAN

Make a Gratitude List in your journal or on a piece of paper, or on your computer? Then read it every morning for the next 30 days before you get out of bed and notice what shows up as you do your day!

EXPRESS YOUR APPRECIATION

So often we get so caught up in our own lives that we take the people around us for granted. I know when I go out of my way to do something that I know my daughter will appreciate, and she either doesn't even acknowledge it, or if she does, she just says an obligatory thanks without making eye contact I feel disappointed, and taken for granted.

One of the ways that she expresses her love and appreciation is by making me the most beautiful cards. I have quite a collection now, and have some in my room, in my office and around the house and I also carry some with me when I travel so that wherever I go, I feel connected to her. I've taught her to express her gratitude in ways that work for her.

Growing up my mum was busy running a business and being an only child I loved to stay at my friend Annie's place for dinner. Her mum (who I called Auntie Jean) used to have a big jug of Lime Cordial and some cup cakes waiting for us after school, and I often stayed on for dinner. For many years I sent her flowers and a card on Mother's Day as she was my 2nd Mum. And I always rang her on her birthday.

She passed away earlier this year but thankfully I called her last December for her 91st birthday. And she was so thrilled to hear from me. She told me it had made her day.

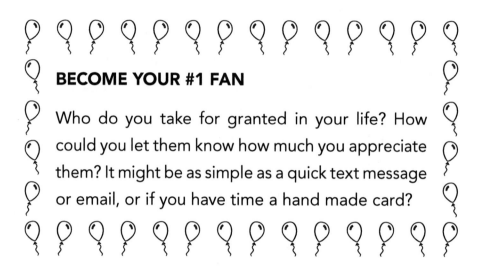

BECOME YOUR #1 FAN

Who do you take for granted in your life? How could you let them know how much you appreciate them? It might be as simple as a quick text message or email, or if you have time a hand made card?

Just like flowers in a garden, our relationships with family members, friends and work colleagues will blossom and grow when we fertilise the soil and let them know how much we appreciate having them our in our lives!

So what are you waiting for? Put this book down right now, and start thanking the significant people in your life! Let them know how much you love and appreciate them!

In Conclusion

Let's revisit the key points in this book

First of all, CONGRATULATIONS on reading this far! That tells me that you are committed to learning more about who you are and learning how to be the best you that you can be and in the process BECOME YOUR #1 FAN (even if you did skip straight to this chapter)

In my experience, I am constantly learning and growing as a person. I learn from all sorts of people. Some of them are my mentors, others are professionals in the personal development industry, while others are people like my beautiful daughter who teaches me how to be a better mum and human being on a daily basis.

And as is probably the case for you, I learn a lot from my stuff ups! In fact I learn the most from my stuff ups or supposed failures. So please know that re-claiming your self esteem and building your self confidence is an ongoing journey. There is no overnight quick fix. As is with anything worth achieving in life, it's a process. And life will present you with all sorts of challenges to test your commitment levels. Years ago you would never have learned to walk and talk if you'd given up after your first attempt, so draw on that perseverance, it's still there inside you.

So let's summarise what we've discussed so far in this book:

- When you were born, you had an infinite amount of Self Esteem and Self Worth.

- As a tiny baby, you didn't know the meaning of the word fail, so didn't have any fear of failure. You interacted with the world around you with a sense of joy, curiosity and spontaneity!

- The first piece of negative feedback that you received changed all of that, and because your brain and language skills were in their infant stages of development, you didn't understand that it was just a behaviour that you were doing or perhaps a negative sibling, so you decided that you were flawed in some way.

- Ever since then you have looked for evidence to support that belief and that in turn created the belief "I'm not good enough".

- You are not your behaviours, you learned those from everyone around you.

- The essence of who you are is magnificent and far stronger and greater than any obstacle that life presents you with.

- Knowing that you are not your behaviours, which behaviours would you like to ditch?

- Acknowledging behaviours that don't serve us, is the first step in discarding them so that we can trying on new some ones.

- Friends, family, teachers, work colleagues will try to put you in a box and label you! Your job is to see it for what it is, and not buy into it. Instead break free and be proud of who you are and love yourself warts and all!

- Dare to dream big and take the actions necessary to make your dreams a reality!

- There is no such thing as failure, only feedback. Feedback is a valuable tool to review, correct and adjust our sails!

- Beware of Dream Busters. They're the ones that don't have the courage to dream. So your courage and commitment to yourself shines a light on their darkness and feelings of inadequacy, and causes them to react badly and try to burst your bubble/dreams.

- Just as toxic, is what we call in Australia the "Tall Poppy Syndrome". Once again, these people don't feel good about themselves, so whenever someone around them dares to stand tall and proud, they feel the need to cut you down to their size, so that they feel more comfortable around you. So keep an eye out for them, and never choose them to share your hopes, dreams and desires with.

- Instead surround yourself with positive, uplifting people who have a healthy self esteem and value you.

- Choose your favourite picture of yourself as a baby and carry it with you all the time as a reminder to be gentle on yourself.

- Journals are a great tool to get to know yourself and build your self esteem.

- Write or give yourself, your friends, family and colleagues at least one compliment every day.

- Celebrate every win, no matter how small!

- Blow up at least one balloon each day by doing something that builds your self esteem and self worth and makes a deposit into your Become your #1 Fan Bank.

- Teach everyone around you to do the same. That way you'll be surrounded by like minded people.

- If someone isn't willing to develop their self esteem, it's their choice. If I were you I'd choose not to spend much time with them from now on; knowing that who we hang out with we become.

- Our brain is like a computer. It believes what we tell it, so be very careful what you tell it!

- Directionalise your language. Focus on what you DO want versus what you don't want.

- Use affirmations to fertilise the soil for your self esteem, self worth and self confidence to blossom and grow.

- Where your attention goes, your energy flows. So what are you going to focus on?

- Try on some new behaviours, attitudes and ways of being?

- Use Winning Words ie; in the past, up until now and yet, to re-program your critical voice and negative thought patterns into positive thought patterns.

- If it's to be, it's up to me! No one else can do it for you. You are in control of your life. So what sort of life do you want?

- Use Transformational Vocabulary to transform your day.

- Nerves are a sign that what you're about to do is important to you. So embrace them, catch your butterflies, put them in a V Formation and breathe deeply as you put up your Performance Bubble.

- Roadblocks are often divine guidance. Your biggest nightmares down the track are always your biggest gift. The quicker you look for the gift, the quicker you'll move through the situation.

- Bounce forward versus back from set backs. Turn the crisis into success.

- Lessons from Geese. Collaboration and Teamwork is the name of the game. Stop trying to achieve things on your own. Ask for help, surround yourself with like minded people and people that have the qualities that you you want to develop.

- Your past does not dictate your future. You do, based on the choices you make.

- Listen to your Intuition. Its never wrong.

- Take the time to express your gratitude. Let those around you know how much you care.

- Make the time to go to your "special place" to feel relaxed and rejuvenated. Meditate, do a guided visualisation or just sit peacefully surrounded by nature.

- Really connect with your Inner Child and allow him/her to come out and play in some way every day.

- You are an extraordinary person with huge gifts to share. So please be brave enough to get out there and share who you really are, and together we will transform our beautiful planet!

As I mentioned earlier, I've created a Membership Website to support you as you make your way through the exercises in this book. By buying this book you're entitled to one months FREE TRIAL to see if you find it valuable.

You'll get to:

~ Connect with me directly
~ Share how you're going with the rest of the members
~ Have access to information that isn't included in the book
~ Learn more ways to Become your #1 Fan

So I hope you take me up on this FREE OFFER and join us.

Membership Website:
www.becomeyournumberonefanmembershipwebsite.com

Once you go to the website above click on the Members Log In Icon to set up your 1 month's free membership. When it asks you for a discount code type in: BOOK OFFER

Aloha,
Kathryn :)

Sources

Begley, Sharon. 2007. Train Your Mind, Change Your Brain: How a New Science Reveals Our Extraordinary Potential to Transform Ourselves. Ballantine Books.

Doidge, N. 2007. The Brain That Changes Itself: Stories of Personal Triumph from the Frontiers of Brain Science. New York:Viking.

Davidson, R. J., J. Kabat-Zinn, J. Schumacher, M. Rosenkranz, D. Muller, S.F. Santorelli, F. Urbanowski, A. Harrington, K. Bonus, and J.F. Sheridan. 2003. Alterations in brain and immune function produced by mindfulness meditation. Psychosomatic Medicine. 65 (4):564–570. http://psyphz.psych.wisc.edu/web/pubs/2003/alterations_by_mindfulness.pdf

Draganski, B., C. Gaser, G. Kempermann, H.G. Kuhn, J. Winkler, C. Buchel, and A. May. 2006. Temporal and spatial dynamics of brain structure changes during extensive learning. Journal of Neuroscience. 26:6314–6317. http://www.ncbi.nlm.nih.gov/pubmed/16763039

Gaser, C. and G. Schlaug. 2003. Brain Structures Differ between Musicians and Non-Musicians. Journal of Neuroscience. 23:9240 - 9245. http://www.jneurosci.org/cgi/content/full/23/27/9240

Maguire, E.A., K. Woolett and H.J. Spiers. 2006. London taxi drivers and bus drivers: A structural MRI and neuropsychological analysis. Hippocampus. 16:1091-1101. http://www.fil.ion.ucl.ac.uk/Maguire/Maguire2006.pdf

Schwartz, J.M. and S. Begley. 2002. The Mind and the Brain: Neuroplasticity and the Power of Mental Force. New York: Harper Collins.

Dr Karl Albrecht. The Art and Science of Common Sense

Langer, E.J. Mindfulness, Addison Wesley, Reading, Massachusetts, 1989

Index

M

N

CPSIA information can be obtained at www.ICGtesting.com
Printed in the USA
LVOW11s1907161213

365574LV00002B/4/P